History (and Pre-)

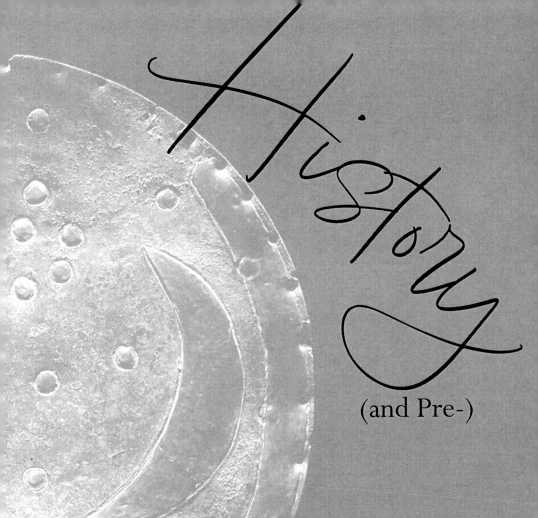

History
(and Pre-)

ALBERT GOLDBARTH

(poems)

LynxHousePress
Spokane, Washington

ACKNOWLEDGMENTS

Some of the poems in this collection previously appeared (occasionally with small differences) in the following publications, the editors of which have my gratitude for their generosity, and for their willingness to accommodate my principled but annoying Luddite sensibility: *The American Review of Poetry; Conduit; December; Gettysburg Review; Lost Horse Press; New Letters; Olney Magazine; Salt; Southern Review; Witness.* None of the poems in this book was created using computer technology; if anything, I have kept these poems as far from the world of screens as possible.

These friends continue to be an inspiration: Sharon Bryan, Stephen Corey, John Crisp, Brian Evans, Nathan Filbert, Kathleen Flenniken, Alice Friman, Michael King, Herb Leibowitz, Joey Lemon, Toni Loeffler, Michael Pointer, Lawrence Raab, Don Selby, Georgia Sutton, Jim Wolken, Wayne Zade. Christopher Howell—as poet, publisher, teacher—is an exemplary presence in the art. Mark Drew and his associates at The Gettysburg Review have helped two generations of writers and readers to be their best.

The cover image is of the "Nebra sky disc" from circa 1600 BC: bronze (and Bronze Age), twelve inches in diameter, and "verified as the oldest confirmed depiction of the cosmos in existence." As a sky map it remains astronomically accurate.

Copyright © 2024 by Albert Goldbarth

FIRST EDITION

Book and Jacket Design: Christine Lysnewycz Holbert
Author Photo: Michael Pointer

LYNX HOUSE PRESS books are distributed by Washington State University Press, wsupress@wsu.edu.

LIBRARY OF CONGRESS CATALOGING-IN-PUBLICATION DATA is available from the Library of Congress.

ISBN 978-0-89924-196-8

CONTENTS

WELCOME

~~Forward~~ Backward   1
A Cosmology   5

HISTORY (AND PRE-)

Summer Rain   9
Variant Narrative   10
Smith   14
Scale Models   16
Going Back Now   18
The Farther Shore   19
The Marvelous Nativity of Jeremiah Dixon, with Culminant Song,
    as Imagined   20
Abe Lincoln's War   22
Gris-Gris Rhapsody   23
Ring   27
Some Realms   28
When Faced with Absence, We Conjure Its Semblance   30
A Handbook of Minimalist Accessing   32
Darwin Invents the Telephone   35
Not Knowing   36
The Weather Report   37
Ovid   38
"Bring the Faces of Your Heritage" Day   39
John Adams (and You Too, Eventually)   41

HISTORY: SNAPSHOTS, 1

The Stars Are Always in the Sky   49
"the cactus allows"   50
Source   51
Memory Lane   52
Aubade   53
"Archaeologists have found mummified maggots"   54
Ozymandias   55
Ravenous   56
Riverdale   57
Song: Until There Were People   58

HISTORY AND ME

Fires   61
Pantheon   64
Fifteen   66
Unwarranted Expectations   68
Ufology [*noun,* "the study of UFOs"]   69
The Golden-cheeked Warbler Breeds Only Within the State of Texas.   72
This Pattern   73
The Song of the Practical   76
Landscape with Peach Trees   77
"To Cure the Tooth-Ach, Take a New Nail, and Make the Gum Bleed with it, and Then Drive It into an Oak"   78
Mediation Poem   80
The Limited Time   83
Wine / OK / Flowers   85
Various Metrics   87
Forever Half-Done   91

Capped   94
My Life Among the Afterlives   98
Smears and Shimmers   105
Clay Pottery Shards: *Pueblo Culture, Pecos*   107
The Golden Flower of Deepest Time   109

HISTORY: SNAPSHOTS, 2

And Snow   115
"So much like a Renaissance figure of Death:"   116
The Systems   117
High Noon   118
Everyday Version   119
After Last Night   120
One Week Before the Divorce Is Final   121
Model-T: A Spin Around the Countryside   122
March. Halt. Kneel. Shoot. [Repeat.]   123
Song: Here   124

HISTORY: COUPLES

Benjamin Waterhouse Hawkins   127
The Power of Less: 129
The Civil War   130
What Evolution Requires   131
The Cleansing   134
Talk: Three Couples   136
Zero: Terror and Lullabye   138
"Y'call someplace Paradise, kiss it goodbye."   140
Mirrors for the World of Human Doing   142

The Story of My Wife's Bow   145
Responsible For   146

HISTORY: SNAPSHOTS, 3

"Oh a clock is so full"   149
A Clock   150
Could Do Worse   151
Remnants   152
Some Fifty Years   153
The Year is 1997. The "Stardusters" Have Already Conquered Venus . . .   154
So Late   155
In the Yellow Fall of Wattage   156
Narrows   157
Because Love Is a Timeless and Distanceless Circle, We'll All Meet
    in Its Center   158

HISTORY: FOUR NARRATIVES

Mary and Mary and Mary   161
Discards   168
"A museum, of sorts, for errors."   174
Notes Toward Two Poems Arguing Each Other, and Toward a Coda That
    Attempts to Favor One   184

"ANACHRONISMS

"Anachronisms   197

When I work on a bone or two, it's very easy to forget
that these are actually people with their own lives and stories.

—Bence Viola, anthropologist, on working with Neanderthal remains

The clear water we drank as thirsty children
still runs through our veins. . . .
We name it the past and drag it behind us,
bag like a lung filled with shadow and song,
dreams of running, the keys to lost names.

—Dorianne Laux, "Dark Charms"

"There's hardly anything left to unpack now."
"Just one or two Antediluvium bones," said Mr. Preemby.
Teddy seized upon one. "This," he said, inspecting it,
is a fossilized rhinoceros thigh-bone from the Crag."
"It's an Antediluvium horse," said Mr. Preemby.
"Forgive me! It's a rhinoceros bone!"
"Horses had rhinoceros bones in those days," said Mr. Preemby. "And the rhinoceroses—! They were incredible. If I had one I shouldn't have anywhere to put it."

—H. G. Wells, Christina Alberta's Father

It is long ago
already.

—Christopher Howell, "The Sea Side"

WELCOME

~~FORWARD~~
BACKWARD

If a sensibility can be said "to look," then mine—not always, but often—looks back. As this book's title indicates, the poems here are all, in some way, informed by that sensibility, although "back" may for some of them be the recent era of typewriters, rotary dial phones, corner mailboxes; in others, the time when "America" meant British colonies; for some, the world of ancient Egypt or, earlier, the Neanderthals or, earlier, pleiosaurs, trilobites; and for others, a mental stretch back to what we call the Big Bang, or to the womb.

In his book *Shooting Stars of the Small Screen,* Douglas Brode distinguishes between the lineage of Herodotus and of Homer—that is, between history as a discipline and history as myth. Some of the poems here owe their allegiance to one of those masters, some to the other.

And the ways in which the poems here make use of "back" also varies. If you read on, you'll encounter poems that ask to address the movement of time as their primary concern; poems that are set, like some historical novel, in a previous time period; and poems that simply use a historical factoid as a springboard into other concerns altogether. And, as in other collections of mine, I've tried to congregate a variety of *kinds* of poems (some brief, but also some lengthy and multipartite; light-hearted, alongside grave; the personal, and also…well, the ones about *you*)—into a single community, in this case one that believes we can't be done with lingering about, and perhaps learning from, what's come before. (Or maybe…all of this is merely an excuse to let some poems that have the promise of congenial mingling gather together.)

A last note. As most books of poetry go, this is *not* a slim volume. I think of its sections as individual chapbooks, each with its own coherence (and variety-within-coherence), organized that way with an apportioned, user-friendly read in mind…and still, I trust these "individual chapbooks" contribute toward a larger and unified whole. That, anyway, is my hope; and I thank you for driving forward now, with rear-view mirror adjusted, into this backward-glancing collection.

for Skyler
past   present   future

A COSMOLOGY

*To climb backwards in the heavens because
we poets live in reverse.*

—Jim Harrison

I struck a light and there it was:
a cat the rabid dog had mauled to death,
and a luckless cardinal with its neck snapped
where the cat had dropped it. Everything here

was something else before. The dog was healthy
once, came running with a pink ball in its jaws
once. Go back far enough,
it was a wolf. The cat was a jungle hunter,

the match was called a lucifer. And my hand
that struck the light?—was a series of cells
in the ribs of a lungfish, all aquiver
with itchy potential. We can never live

in the land of before; the arrow of spacetime
won't allow that. But it calls to us, the way
the fabled always does. We had *some* name
for the cardinal before the Catholic Church.

And Satan, just like the match, was Lucifer once.
But that was before. If there wasn't "before,"
there wouldn't be an "after." "After": where we live.
It's becoming the next "before" this second.

HISTORY (AND PRE-)

SUMMER RAIN

The actor boasts: in his current film
the deforestation of ancient Mayan territory
will teach our twenty-first century a lesson.

Not a saving one, I fear. We're heading so rapidly
into the future that we're overtaking the past. Any day now
Rome will tumble, the lions will hunt and fuck in the streets.

. . .

When I was angry at her I was angry at everything,
just like when I was a child. When I nibbled her fingertip,
lovingly, I was sucking my thumb by proxy again.

How readily we're drawn back in time.
"Summer Rain" is the poem by Chase Twitchell
I quickly read as "Sumerian."

VARIANT NARRATIVE

From *Ancient Inventions*, James and Thorpe: "By the fourth millennium B.C. the urban civilization of Sumer, in southern Iraq, had developed a complex accounting system, involving 250 different types of [baked clay] tokens. From top to bottom are the tokens symbolizing

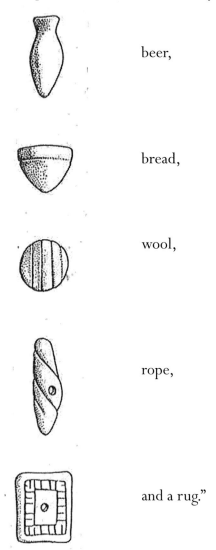

beer,

bread,

wool,

rope,

and a rug."

Come my [heart's?] desire, my [heart?]
my [loins?] burn[s] like a furnace,
my man of the oxen strength, I have
aplenty of beer, aplenty of ripe dates,
now we must [this line is missing]

and take the pleasures of [animals: gazelles?]
beneath the stars, the night is
[missing] and in the morning
we will take our bread together,
we will greet [the sun?] together

but, ah! my enemy is at the door,
the woman of [activity: carding?] wool
is at the door, she is a snake,
my love, she is a [unclean]-thing,
do not [consort?] with her, my love

or I or I [several lines are missing]
[image for striking a blow]
and I then [an image: bind with rope?]
[missing lines] a [unclean?]-thing
should not be permitted to live

my love, my man of obsidian eyes,
and I then and I then
[some verb] her body in the rug
like [a shroud?] and carry it
beneath the stars to the river

Ho, shield-brother! I have here
A great jest to share. Undo your hitches
And join me a while, with this beer.
Do you remember those two bitches
I was eager to make disappear?

One was as soft as warm bread
From the baking-stone,
One was a very lioness in bed.
But neither would leave me alone,
They were a torment in my head,

And so. . . . You know how we say "pull
(You will laugh over this with me
Until the stars go down!) the wool
Over somebody's eyes? Well, one she-
Devil I invited to visit my door, and the fool

Had no idea I did the same
With her rival. When they found
Each other, ho!, they bristled, they came
To blows. *Guards!* I shouted—who arrived
    and bound
The two in ropes, and led them off in shame.

Do you see?
I was free
Of both of them! I was free,
I could forget
The past, I could fly like the legendary carpet!

I meet Tim at the microbrewery on First,
to parse the simmering divorce talk
of our friends Simone and Dieter.
As you might imagine, their stories don't
align. It turns out "history" is another name

for "version." One's the breadwinner;
one keeps house. One's from a loving family;
one survived a sewer of adders. Tim says that
the universal law is: *No one story
is one story.* Right. An ancient adage

goes "It's not the same hill to the sheep
and to the wolf." Tim: "Or to the shepherd."
Me: "Or the richfuck lord who owns the flock."
With only Adam and Eve in the world,
there was already more than a single world.

"And there have been people strung up,
lynched, for claiming a variant narrative."
This is all moving us far away
from our bickering friends—in this poem.
In another poem, somewhere, perhaps not. Tayanna

joins our table, and contributes her astronomer's
exempla. "We say 'the man in the moon.'
Traditionally, in Mexico, it was a rabbit.
And stars! One culture sees The Battle Chariot;
another sees The Tapestry."

SMITH

A century and a half ago George Smith, then a printing firm apprentice in Bloomsbury, took to visiting the collection of ancient Mesopotamian clay tablets in the British Museum. Eventually he taught himself to read them (no minor feat) and came to realize that one, which we now know is a section of the famously seminal "Epic of Gilgamesh," told the story of a man instructed by his God to build a boat that would save him and his from an earth-drowning flood . . . this, from roughly 400 years before what is the oldest surviving version of the Judeo-Christian Old Testament. A contemporary of Smith's reported this scene at the normally cloister-like, hushed Museum: "He said, 'I am the first man to read that after 2,000 years of oblivion.' Setting the tablet on the table, he jumped up and rushed about the room in a great state of excitement, and, to the astonishment of those present, began to undress himself!" To which Neil MacGregor, current Director of the Museum, adds: "This really was a discovery worth taking your clothes off for."

>   Because to you it looks like the thousands of skritches
>   a tiniest bird, a thumbling bird, would track
>   across the sands, but I am literate in this script,
>   oh my my lord, yes I can read across
>   two thousand years, as if my eyes might pierce the gloom
>   inside a well two thousand miles deep. Because
>   these words have been hardened in fire. Because
>   we raise hosannahs heavenward and what gets showered
>   down in counterbalance is eternal waters, surely
>   a deluge of waters, oh my oh my, because the very highest
>   of mountains have been aswim, because the sharpest snow peaks
>   of the highest mountains have once served

as the nuptial bed and the death bed of Leviathan, oh
my waistcoat seems to have gone astray, my waistcoat
is flying, my my, is a dove flung from the calloused, launching
tenderness of Noah's palm—*unhand me, sirs,*
unhand me! I have witnessed how
at the public dissection of corpses male and female
at the medical school, the first of the body's offerings
in its posthumous existence is a pouring
forth of waters, how the organs of our dear devoted interiors
are islands in a flood, indeed how we carry
the flood all the days of our lives,
and my underwaistcoat too disappears
in my ecstasy, disappears in my understanding
of time between one world of gods and the next
 —*unhand me I say, you cheap grotesque, you London Zoo*
baboon, I shall see that you NEVER receive
official permission to board the Ark, oh
my my, I have been baptized in the deeps of a Babylonian clay
and consecrated in punchmarks of cuneiform,
oh my shoes sail off like coracles over a rolling sea,
I fear not, I possess oracular power and I fear not,
I shall gladly welcome my watery end
as naked as when my mother's water
broke—her oceanic water broke—
at my beginning.

SCALE MODELS

She can't *stand* what she calls "guru hooey":
"the All in the One," "the cosmic round
in the mustard seed." So oopily goopily
mystical, a vision so irrelevant to *here*,
where we sit with the garden soil
darkening our undernails, *here*, where we stand
with the sweet swamp-flimmer of sex juice
rising up from our fingers, *here*,
with the candle wax, the taxes, the basketball, politics . . . i.e.,
"reality"—as imaged in the detailed scale model

of the entire Han empire (rivers
of flowing mercury, a sky map
constellated with pearls, an aviaryful
of birds in silver and gold) discovered in the emperor's tomb,
boxed away beneath the earth, and holding,
representationally, the hundreds of thousands of miles of Earth
and Heaven of the emperor's rule: a version
of that region in the brain "where your entire body
is registered, a mini-you of living electrochemical
cartography." One day

she holds her hand to the light, to the simple
lozenge of light that enters a kitchen window.
Her hand, her opened hand—that's all.
So tiny a fragment of the universe! Yet here
are the beds of the Tigris and the Euphrates,
faint but discernible, the salt plain

and the fertile plain, and the mound
not unlike her vaginal flesh,
and the mound where the ancient temples were established
to stare at the ancient gods.

GOING BACK NOW

There are pathways in the ancient world
—pilgrim trails, caravan trails—used
so often, and with such continuity, over centuries,
their textures have been worn
to a seamless sheen, so that you walk
or drive your sheep or ride your camel
over a ribbon of pure patina; just as there
are statues touched for luck
by so many generations, that their breasts
or lips or penises—whatever point is symbolic
of beneficence—are worn down to the general
idea of breasts or lips or penises,
individuation having been gentled away,
over time, toward something deeper. We're

too new, to have created anything
so temporally soulful; the repetitive tracks
of to-fro cellphone zinging or
communications satellites can't do it, or anyway
not yet. But we get the feeling, don't we, that
the limited units we call our lives partake of something
larger and immemorial: our lazy, easy spooning
in the marriage bed one morning is the edge
of a continuum of likeness going back
now for millennia. Once, in Arizona,
I could see the sun and the dissipating
cool of night combine to lift a steam
from the bodies of cattle: ancient
braziers, and their ancient embers,

Nineveh, Carthage, Pompeii.

THE FARTHER SHORE

If you ask the ancient Egyptians, we're *all* cicadas
ready to sing again on the farther shore of Nothing.
There are tombs of theirs with toilets included, to be used
in the afterlife. Whatever interim dormancy
he traveled after dying, uncle Len
must have arrived, at last, at someplace architected
in affinity with everything he'd been already; auntie Evie dreams him
composing his wiry frame in the chair on his heavenly porch
at dusk and, just as always, studying the hazy shapes
of jellyfish that swim up from his shag tobacco then vanish
into the darkening heavenly evening sky. As sappy
as that is, its gist is true: two points in time
(say, *here* and *there*) can be contemporized
by likeness. An empress's stables-boy lover was slaughtered
and buried with her; as if death were merely an inconvenient
moment of interruption.

THE MARVELOUS NATIVITY OF JEREMIAH DIXON, WITH CULMINANT SONG, AS IMAGINED

Of Dixon, the Dictionary of National Biography *notes intriguingly that he was "said to have been born in a coal mine," but then leaves it to the reader's imagination to supply a plausible explanatory circumstance.*

—Bill Bryson

It's true that I don't know
if she was hiding from some man
(a father? a lover?) with a leather strop
in his hand and a jackal leer in his eye;
or supplying baskets of cider, ham, and johnnycake
for a few of the men who were laboring
in the shakily candle-lit dark
of what they called "the toe of the goddamn sock"
—the farthest, lowest point; or simply following
a caprice: to curl up, fetally,
as close to the magma heart
of Mother Earth herself
as coal mine verticality allowed, and there
deliver her daughter (she thought it would be
a daughter).
         What I do know
is that he was suddenly here,
amid the great
bituminous or anthracite potential
for becoming fire—fire
that was stored in the veins of that cavity

in the planet; and so he could claim,
in a sense, two wombs,
and so two births: one flesh, one mineral;
and I believe
that all the canaries
the miners carry in there as a precaution,
cleared their golden throats and offered up a benison.

ABE LINCOLN'S WAR

is another name for the Civil War, as if
he felt proprietary about this strife,
or Eisenhower's, Churchill's, and I wonder
if everybody must have a war, if everybody
must be eponymous with a war, if only a little war
in the body, with the Bull Run in the heart,
the Iwo Jima in the suffering groin, I wonder
if Lou Gehrig's disease is quiet tonight or making
crafty plans in Brian's body, Tourette's,
Alzheimer's, I'd rather be attached to spangles
in the sky like those defining the Van Allen Belt
than own the islets of Langerhans, but I imagine
everybody can lay claim to their part
of outer space and to their part of the inner dark
in us where the rival factions hunker down
for the night behind their hills and wait
for the cannon to wheel up for another day,
a day in your body, a day in my body,
a war a nation declares in the names of all of us
whether we like it or not, do you remember Nixon's war,
the Children's Crusade, an ongoing battle
in Brian whether he likes it or not, and sometimes
little moments of joy that scratch across the sky
of our lives in circuits like Halley's Comet.

GRIS-GRIS RHAPSODY

If you'd witnessed Tyrona the slave-child running
in a blind-eyed shit-pantsed terror,
in a stampede exactly the size of a single
bullwhipped eight-year-old girl, across the lawn
of the mansion at Royal and Hospital Streets
in New Orleans, in 1833, with her mistress
Madame Delphine Lalaurie, the wife
of Dr. Louis Lalaurie, repeatedly cracking the lash
—with the sound of a quarter-inch pine plank snapping—
across the girl's back, drawing blood, drawing gurgled
animal sounds from her lungs, until she ran back in
to the house, to the roof, to its edge of eaves,
and kept on into the air and down to shatter
on the flagstones of the courtyard,
a piece of garbage the color of eggplant,
bone, and organ meats . . .
                            then you too might
require the consolation, not to mention the protection,
that only a gris-gris of the highest angelic echelon
provides, and you would catsneak out of the compound,
under the star signs of the Voodoo gods that were scattered like grain
—like grain on fire—against the night, and make your way
to the most effective practitioner of those ministerial
Haitian arts, the Mystic Doctor Yah-Yah; and he,
for a few scrimped coins and a skimpy chicken
still warm, maybe even still twitching, under your arm,
would reach with great grave ceremony into one
of the tiny nests of knotted-up hair he styled

into the vastly mazey bough of hair upon his head,
and withdraw a tiny oilskin pouch of his Guaranteed Cure-All Mix
of sulphur, jimson weed, and honey, which you were instructed
to sip at the full moon from a glass that was rubbed
against a black cat with one white foot, and trouble
would be warded off, as promised, for the month.
                                        Or
if your man [or if your woman], the one who turns your will
to a sugary jelly that pools in your breast
and chokes up your gizzard, your All, your One and Only Flower
Down in the Love Gulley, suddenly is discovered
in the hamhocks shack as naked as a newborn rat
with the equally naked [fill in name], and there isn't any more earth
below your feet or reason to wake up . . .
                                        then you might consult
the estimable Conjuror Jack, whose famously potent
(and pricey: twenty 1850s dollars) Hoodoo Love Charm
was a beef heart "scented with spices and perfumes
and wrapped in a white crape. It was known to be
infallible if left on a doorstep," and Conjuror Jack himself
had one such beef heart hung above his bed
in the house on old Treme Street, and his wife reported
that it had fallen down from that honored amuletic place
three days before his death.
                            Or if you were (or were anything
like) that "wealthy merchant of New Orleans"
(because, although we often forget it, that time and place
held tangled borders: there were black slaveowners,
just as there were white elites who were crazy
for joining—-clandestinely—Voodoo orgies) whose youngest son

had been arrested (though innocent) for some crime
lost to the history books: innocent, but
with circumstantial evidence stacked convincingly;
if you were that desperate parent, then . . .
                              you too might visit
the flimsy shanty on Lake Pontchartrain
where the Voodoo Queen, Marie Laveau herself, lived,
and for payment not only in cash but
also a cottage on St. Ann Street nearby Congo Square,
she would place three Guinea peppers in her mouth
while praying feverishly for an hour, and then secretly deposit them
under the bench of the presiding judge: and the boy
would be acquitted.
              And you, my friends,
my dear ones, living in your own—whether secret
or public—oversaturated versions of fear and despair,
my sleepless and fretting ones (don't tell *me*
that you've never been sleepless), laboring, laboring
under awareness of the official inevitability
of death that's in your brain stem like the curled worm
in the silt of the tequila bottle, you
at the base of the ramparts of night
that are architected to vast inhuman scale, with
your worry over political fracas pincering away
another brain-speck every time you allow the news inside
your skull, with the screens and the algorithms
that own you, with the mortgage and the colleagues
and the oncology wing and the climate and the species death
and the bomb in the faux Coke can in the bus
at the airport, you with the ten-thousand pull-apart

burdens of love . . . you too
                            will seek assurance
in whatever juju-luck your culture sanctions, you
who sometimes feel *there isn't any more earth beneath your feet
or reason to wake up*, you will understandably
pilgrimage to the marriage counselor,
the family therapy counselor, the 12-step program,
with their therapeutic mumbo jumbo panacea magic,
you will try to divine the stock market tips
as somebody else might study the future
in blemishes on a ram's guts, you will count the titrate drippings
of the chemo, you will tell the beads of the rosary
of high blood pressure pills that quiets your days,
and cling to Jesus, or cling to the guru's story
of your past lives, and you will implore,
and you will beseech, and you will bend to the knees
you carry in your mind, and you will continue,
continue, continue to do so, benefitting sometimes,
sometimes not, but investing in these
until the heart-of-hearts you've placed
in regal prominence above your bed
gives up and drops to the floor.
Amen.

RING

She's still asleep; her ring, left overnight
out on the ledge above the sink.
"Asleep"—how far away is that,
is it deeper than coal, is it higher than the blue
of Pluto's frosts? He's seen the repro
of a ring from the ancient city
some believe was Plato's model for Atlantis,
it's a dredged-up ring of gold
"with an unreadable inscription
which appeared to be related to Etruscan and to Greek,"
but it *isn't* Etruscan or Greek, or anything
we can translate. If we found the lost Atlantis
on the dark side of the moon, would it be stranger than the dictionary
we keep in us on the dark side of the brain?

We sleep—its pages open.
We wake—it shudders and closes.

SOME REALMS

How many tons of dust are falling
from space right now, down distance
only the astrophysicist wizards could compute,
how much of the black star-shot enormity
above us can our eyes absorb and our brains
comprehend as we slog along on the bottom of that
overhead infinity? This is why
I understand Atlantis is a metaphor

for living here, on the surface of the Earth,
with my poems, and my car keys, and my worries
about the lab test and the terrorist alert,
with my friends and my dreams and my alarm clock
and my wife with her rhinestone owl brooch.
An eel the length of a limousine weaving slinkily
through the vendors of the marketplace, with a single
diaphanous fin on its upside, billowing like ink . . .
whatever that might have been in Atlantis, I assure you

its correspondence is here, among us.
In fact all of the wonders and all of the savage depravities
we've attributed to that continent
—I remember a story about the ritual
children's dance around the bubble fountains
in the plaza; I remember a story about the public
flaying of enemy warriors, and how those skins
upon removal were fastened as flags
that ripple on top of staffs set into the walls—

are really like the subvocalized words
beneath our own everyday speech.
As for the Atlanteans . . . did they think there was something

under them too, something that worked
like a sunken world? Yes: they believed in a realm
they called the Subconscious, where wavery likenesses
of themselves enacted their urges. To the extent

that we've inherited a concept of Atlantis, we've
inherited a second-hand idea of this realm. The way
that the early legs of ambulatory whales are still
tucked into the flesh of the whales in our seas . . .
we carry a little subconscious
where the twins of us lead their own lives.

WHEN FACED WITH ABSENCE, WE CONJURE ITS SEMBLANCE

The palaestra,

Pompeii's great stadium, had been surrounded
by trees before Vesuvius blew, though

archeologists only found an empty ashen plain
—until they filled the spaces the roots had left

with plaster, so the kind and size
and variety of the trees, tall plane trees,

took on chalky definition. Plaster:
as if the ghost of a tree

might be as hard as the tree.

...

Halfway across the world from there, the whale
is being hunted, larger than anything

in their village, larger than anything a man
could ever aspire to be, the flukes alone are greater

than the dreams of a king. And so the soul of the whale
is asked for forgiveness, and the whale's death

is given a song, perhaps if the entire village joins
its voices, the sound will be as large as the whale

and rule the sky instead of the sea
   —as if the ghost can counterbalance the body

if it's made out of song.

A HANDBOOK OF MINIMALIST ACCESSING

> . . . *a nimbus of dust*
>
> —David Wojahn

Belzoni's methods were thuggish ("he thought nothing
of smashing open sealed tombs with a battering ram")
but his daredevil gumption
can't be quibbled with: once, he leaped over the rail
into the Nile, wrestling—on his own (he'd worked
as a circus strongman in London)—an overboard
stone obelisk back to the barge. In Egypt's
Valley of the Kings, James Bruce survived an attack
by tomb-robbers, who attempted to bury the man
alive, under a rockslide.
     Ah, the risk,
the romance, the nape-hair-raising legendary tales
of archeology!—of consorting with banditti,
bats, and scorpions, for the pleasure of seeing
a glint of objects peeking from muck
at the bottom of the well of time, and feeling
the shock, the almost defibrillator shock,
that enters your body through touching something untouched
over 3,000 years.
     Rawlinson was dangled by rope
to a cliff 160 dizzying feet above the valley
called "the landscape of the gods," overseeing the ancient road
to Babylon, and there—as the vast, vast wind
beat at his small, small body, and all of the dust

in Assyria seemed to scour him—he dutifully
transcribed the fourteen columns of self-congratulatory
praise that Darius, King of the Persians, had ordered chiseled
into the rock. As the nerdy guy in the eighth-grade
science movies always said with a scripted chuckle,
"Kids, don't try *this* one at home, haha!"
                                                                     And yet

we do, we do successfully,
in our minimalist way: Bill Bryson tells us,
"Run a finger along a dusty shelf and you
are drawing a pattern very largely in old skin":
a small (but real) hands-on, immediate,
archeologized intimacy
with the world of the past. It's like

                            . . .

when I was sixteen, maybe seventeen, nearly anything,
a scene in a novel or movie, a song, an ambulance siren
making distance palpable through its intimation
of tragedy, could—when vibratory alliance
with my psyche was prepared for this—awaken
in me an openness to ecstasy and related
emotional overspilling. The nighttime sky
especially could do it, could cue it,
and even today—and I believe you know
your own not dissimilar versions—a walk
beneath a full moon's opulence will suddenly
resensitize my mind back to those earlier times,
and the glory and vertigo-terror

of the heavens will descend on me once more, and replenish
that earlier überresponse to the very idea
of being alive, of bearing the weight of being even
an insignificant unit of those fires and that emptiness,
and (despite the sci-fi film where the astronaut
opens her eyes and screams a scream that bleeds
straight off the edges of the screen, having stared
for too long at the implacable face of Eternity itself) I want
to risk the fear of the vacuum, risk the sear
of the radiation, risk the need of the brain
for a furrowed brain-sized hazmat suit,
and rise up there to the spectra of where
we began, and broil and fly and be baptized
down to my DNA, inside that first and final
Mystery.
        I can't, of course. And neither
can you. But I do know a trick I learned
from Bill Bryson: "Every year the Earth accumulates
thirty thousand metric tons of 'cosmic spherules'
—space dust." If your housekeeping skills resemble mine,
you can write your name in the stars.

DARWIN INVENTS THE TELEPHONE

In Chile, Darwin walked on mountain pinnacles
12,000 feet above the sea—and there
discovered seashells in the ashy dirt.
A puzzle. Some were only the size of his thumbnail.
Others, he could hold to his ear
and still make out, clear though faint,
the language of the ocean.

...

This was of course before the invention
of smartphones and Zooming, before
we discovered "entanglement" in the quantum realm.
But here was the ocean none the less,
Well hello there, on top of a mountain.

NOT KNOWING

One telling example of the growing success of religious censors in the twenties is the contrast between two editions. The frontispiece of the 1922 edition features a portrait of Charles Darwin. By 1926, Darwin had been removed and replaced with a drawing of the human digestive system.

—Susan Jacoby on *Biology for Beginners* by Truman Moore

The perfect emblem: organs unconnected
to anything—certainly not to a theory;
not to something like a mouth, that could speak;
or like the genitalia. Once, in a town in downstate
Illinois, I saw a pile of books they'd torched:
a thickly laden smoke rose up in exactly
that shape, an esophagus linked to a stomach;
then it floated off, just one more cloud,
just one more disappearance. "The ordinary habits
of the ostrich," Darwin says, "are familiar
to everyone." *To everyone*, Darwin assumes.
So once again, I've failed him,
who trusted that we know, and care to know more yet.
The only image I have in my head is *its* head,
hidden in the sand: another perfect emblem.

THE WEATHER REPORT

Reading in Darwin: what's a lovely vista
(say "a forest, which in the grandeur
of its parts could not be exceeded," or that view from the hills
"where the sky and the water vie with each other in splendour")
is simultaneously tortured: and he looks,
like a surgeon, into the rifts and he witnesses the war
of heave and resistance—strangled and distended and twisted
deeply—to the lava below. And maybe this duality
is everywhere, once we're thinking that way.
                                                   One of them
knows it's over. The other is certain of its continuing.
Where is Darwin now, tonight, to chart this
strenuous meteorology?—two vanes in bed,
an inch apart or less, yet each is pointing
to the push of a separate weather.

OVID

In the grassier hills surrounding B.C. Rome,
a shepherd sings to his flocks, "Oh,
come along, pretty-ones, honey-ones, loves," as if
they're people—as if, in the dazzle of noontime light,
they shapeshift into people who he cares about;
and at night the stars turn into vaguely
human forms or, even more amazingly
and vaguely, into gods . . . the borders
separating states of existence seem to be
so fluid here in a world still touched by the old
Greek stories: the painfully beautiful, solipsistic
boy who turns into a flower; the girl whose skin
transgresses into bark, and her feet grow rooted,
and her fingers bud. . . . Maybe, despite the antiquity,

these are the stories of my friends and yours
—despite the sensibility gap
of yellow crime scene tape, the whole botanica
of available gizmo earbuds, boob jobs, gene
replacement therapies, virus firewalls…these
are still the stories of change, of ancient metamorphoses.
For instance: in those B.C. hills, a shepherd slips into
a twilight drowse, and into the dream he often has of becoming
a wolf: the fangs, the active lope, the hunger.
And a wolf—as in those stories—wakes: unhackle
by unhackle it smooths its fur; and feels
the painful burst of opposable thumbs; and cries out
in confusion; and stands; and turns into a man.

"BRING THE FACES OF YOUR HERITAGE" DAY

Exactly one year after the first expedition, the team again left Peking for the Gobi. . . . Making camp in mid-afternoon, they scattered to look for fossils. By nightfall, everyone had his own dinosaur skull.

—*Sean B. Carroll, on Roy Chapman Andrews's 1925 paleontology journey*

In class, one woman has her hair so intricately
beaded and braided and butter-sheened, her head
looks like the planter holding a great voluptuous
flowering shrub, and the feeling is
that generations of royal African ancestry extend
in an equally colorful—albeit ghostly—line
behind her, head after head, shrubs down
unbroken to the infinity-point, while the man beside her
holds in front of his face, like a shield,
the photocopied and copier-enlarged face
of his father after a day in the foundry,
sweat mixed into the grime enough so that
the flash of the camera suddenly gives
the weariness a nearly heraldic blaze, and this,
he says, is representative of his father's
father as well, and of *his* father, all of them
toiled against a backdrop of the forty-foot
pour of molten metal and hornet-swarms of sparks
that were a day (or a night) in the foundry,
and I'm wondering if the rules of kinship
attached to this game allow me to raise
an image of Keats's death mask or a picture

of Marianne Moore in her famous tricorn hat
as family I look back to, even at the risk
of hubris, and if so, perhaps I'll claim
some unknown dweller of the caves who first
said "star" or "pain" or "menstrual blood"
in a language that was only in this moment
becoming a language, and who took his role
or her role in the ritual where the animal skulls
were worn like masks, like alternate heads,
and the animal sounds were made in the midst
of duplicating animal sex and of dying, and perhaps
it isn't difficult now to imagine the birds
acknowledging the lineage of dinosaur skulls
they came from, isn't difficult to ride the escalator
down, and down again, inside us, to the original
electrochemical yowza and good-golly in the waters of Earth
the first of the unicellular mothers and fathers of us
went forth from, and exuberantly multiplied.
How far, how unspeakably distant, in time
did those dinosaur eggs they discovered
seem to Chapman and his men?
Nobody in 1925 even *knew* that dinosaurs reproduced
by eggs. Yet . . . there they were, undeniably,
the start and the end of all mystery.
Well, no, not the end . . . in two of them
the men could see the bones of dinosaur embryos.
Dinosaur embryos!
Like dioramas of time at work.
There isn't an end, there are only our parents
shrubbed and foundried, tongue upon tongue,
succession after succession.

JOHN ADAMS (AND YOU TOO, EVENTUALLY)

Six states regarded themselves as "three-sided," which meant that their citizens considered their western boundaries still open . . . until they reached the Pacific Ocean.

—A. J. Langguth, *on mindset among the original thirteen states*

1.

One night in September, going out in the dark to view a comet, Adams tripped over a stake in the ground and ripped his leg open to the bone.

—David McCullough

    A shame we've so degraded
    "amazing" and "awesome" by now, but really
    the unfathomable grandeur of a comet
    —grandeur, and terror too,
    and mystery—have always been beyond
    articulation. Of the comet
    in myth . . . well, I don't need to elaborate,
    you can fill in the gods
    and the great heart-battering epics
    where that dragon's-tail of fire
    is the central event. Of the comet
    in art (see "Bayeaux Tapestry") . . .
    in Western science . . . as portent
    ("thought to be omens of war,
    of famine, earthquake, flood, drought, sickly herds,
    sterility, the plague, the end of the world" or
    "may bring fortune and peace") . . . John Adams

is learned and knows all of this. He
reads. His personal library "numbered
3,200 volumes"—in a time when a single book
might possibly have meant a month of its travel
by ship and another full day by carriage.
He said in *Thoughts on Government*: "It shall be the duty
of legislators . . . to cherish the interests
of literature and the sciences." In his copy
of Mary Wollstonecraft's *French Revolution*
(he read it twice), his marginal comments ran
to around 12,000 words—that's
how many separate quill dips?
(As if helping create a nation weren't enough.)
His mind was hungry. And so
in 1811—at seventy-five—when he's
called out to view a comet,
to meet this doom-bringer naked face to naked face
(or to greet this celestial wonder-bearer in homage), to

shit God shit God oh God oh Jesus oh oh my Lord
            the sear
and *miles* of overhead apparition disappear
into six ripped-open inches of body.

2.

He could be priggish. Raspy.
He bristled. "Cold and reserved,"
said Benjamin Rush of their first meeting.
He was unforgiving, often,

of everyday human softness and foibles
—of our small dissemblings and lassitudes,
our talent for rascality. He turned all pinched and waspish
when confronted with those. They said that
"he judged harshly." This included himself;
he had few illusions to comfort him
about what he (and we) were like. But
listen, he never once accepted a bribe.
He never sidestepped the considerable wisdom
of his conscience, or made a tool of anyone else's.
Of all of the "founding fathers," only Adams
never owned a slave. (And Abigail fought for the right
of an African-American boy she admired
to be admitted to school.) When Adams enters a room
it's not with easy sugared blandishments
on his lips . . . but more importantly, words
like "honor" and "probity" come to mind.
Eventually Benjamin Rush becomes
an affectionate friend; if you and I will only give Adams
a similar leisure in which to make his acquaintance,
we can see him

kneeling, lost and broken, at his daughter's bedside
—Nabby; she was forty-six—before the doctors entered the room
and ushered him out, and began on that day in that time
before anesthetics to cut away
her right breast.
              ". . . brought a marked change
in Adams. He became more mellow,
more accepting and forgiving."

                             He said,
"I find my imagination . . . roaming in the Milky Way,
those mighty orbs, and stupendous orbits of suns,
planets, satellites, and comets, which compose
the incomprehensible universe"—open
by now to ecstasy.

                             3.

Let's enter this scene. You and I can join him
on a hill top, on an autumn night
when the piled leaves of rural Massachusetts
billow over the slope below like a gold and umber tide.
We too, like him, have been a hard pit at the center
—ingnarled, unyielding—and not the ripe flesh,
not the liquid sweetness or the skin
completely welcoming of the sun. His stories,
yours, and mine, each have their separate details
[fill in yours, here: _____] but the inner limitation
(call it rectitude, on a positive day; or
simply pissy naysaying, on a negative) is
so shared, it's like the handshake of a brotherhood.
And even so . . .
                    I think of those original
thirteen states. One side of four was open
endlessly. Bison,
Native American gods, a great tree the circumference
of a governor's house's rotunda,
pterosaur skeletons, a dolphin's arc . . .

Yellowstone . . . Hollywood. . . .
Anything is possible. Let's look up
to the highest scrim of the atmosphere
that the techno-billionaires pay out the ass to be flown to.
Let's stretch raptured on our backs and face
the mystery-space where the comets are birthed.
And then? Let's breathe beyond even that
—there isn't any barrier on this side of us—
then beyond even that.

HISTORY: SNAPSHOTS, 1

THE STARS ARE ALWAYS IN THE SKY,

even in the brightest day. We know this.
Still, it's startling, walking out at night
—as if they've been freshly created.

Like newborns, I think.
The atoms were there all along,
although we didn't see them.

• • •

the cactus allows
the wind to be a flagellant

   and so we invent the thorned whip for ourselves

• • •

the pond allows
the moon to be rocked to rest

   and so we invent the cradle

• • •

whatever we've done
we've done in companionship with the earlier ones

   I'm writing this
because the willow dipped down to scribble the stream

SOURCE

The dowser holds the willow switch and it dips,
it dips, it points the way back
to the hidden water; the mother; the source.

...

Even in its dying, if you lift a salmon
gently, cupping it gently, you feel its need to turn
like a compass needle, to face its being spawned.

...

The bullet doesn't want the enemy's flesh.
It wants to use that flesh, so it can lay back down
in the earth, where it came from.

MEMORY LANE

"But I *had* to: he was such an asshole!"
Yes. Although the he of that story carries around
a different, and an equally persuasive, version.

Nobody wants to live with regret. And after
a little creative revision, almost nobody does.

We visited here, we traveled there: The air
in the seacoast villages, we said, was almost as solid
as stairs of salt a man could walk up—and we liked
the sound of our saying it. We donated
to the alms-box that was handcarved into a great
fantasmagoria of saints. We helped the elderly woman
purchase her medication. We hired a hot,
salon-waxed hooker and paid her extra for a special
deviation. We know: we have videos. We scaled
the heights and we drilled to the depths.

How often we do what we do so we
can remember it that way later.

AUBADE

We wake; we may as well have been asleep
two thousand, three thousand years in the darkness.
I think of "mummy wheat,"

the colloquial term archeologists use.
All of that time in the dust of the pharaohs, and still
when we plant it, here in the everyday light of the world,

it remembers and grows.

. . .

Archaeologists have found mummified maggots
curled up inside mummified human skulls
—like fossils of thoughts;

like fossils of thoughts
of the kind where the Emperor

plans to invade his neighbors.

OZYMANDIAS

What a week! His definitive book
on Disney animation needed revising,
a doctor's appointment, in-laws visiting: the works!

*If the whole of the 4½ billion years of the Earth
could be seen as a single day* . . . you know what sprinkle
of dander we would be. "The Ozymandias thing."

He never completed his book. The doctor
showed him the proof of a gray half-inch
inside him that was bigger than the book.

In one of the old cartoons an animal is walking across the fallen snow,
continuously marking it with pawprints—that
its tail, just as continuously, erases out of existence.

RAVENOUS

We're hungry. We know our eyes routinely
gourmandize the sexual possibilities of passersby,
the heart snacks on Parnassus
up to its snowbelt-of-a-crown,
then licks the minarets of Jerusalem for dessert, and still
it isn't filled, it isn't anything but continuous

consumption. I can hear this in the voices
of even my mildest friends. The fingertips:
a mouth. Of course the genitals: a mouth.
And the knees we fall to, on the nave's floor.
There was a church once, in the Holy Land, that
allowed the faithful to kneel and kiss the True Cross,
each Good Friday, until one wild-eyed worshipper

bit a souvenir sliver out, and swallowed.

RIVERDALE

They no longer know what's in my poems.
Not that it's special knowledge;
it's merely disappearing. K didn't know
today who Archie is, and Betty and Veronica;
yesterday, the story of Bluebeard; Easter Island;
Plato's cave. It's all becoming mulch
for a future knowledge I can't imagine.

Tonight I walked below the moon, reciting the moon's
departing litany of names from Diana to Armstrong,
Aldrin, Collins. Robinson Crusoe
and Ernie Banks and the Ronettes and
the Berlin Wall were sinking in a real Bermuda Triangle
that was lost, itself, in the grip of a metaphorical
Bermuda Triangle. One hand lifted above the water:

Jughead's, I thought. And then it was gone.

SONG: UNTIL THERE WERE PEOPLE

    no stone was a stepping stone
    no stone was a millstone
    no stone was a lintel stone
    no stone was a whetstone
    no stone was a kidney stone
    no stone was a flagstone
    no stone was a birth stone
    no stone was a tombstone

HISTORY AND ME

FIRES

"My psyche, back in those days, was like skin in a burn ward."

That's what I wrote, and I liked it. It was *good*.

But I was ashamed of it, I hadn't earned it, I had no right to that image. Me?—who always sees that the match flame doesn't creep close to my fingers when the recalcitrant fuse on the firework takes too long to light on a purpling July Fourth evening? *Me?*

So I returned to that line of my poem, to revise it, which was *my* work in this world. Somebody else reads the gas meter. Somebody flings her rhinestoned cloak away and struts, to the *tut-tut-tut* of a snare drum, into the tiger's cage. Somebody plays the snare drum. Somebody manufactured the snare drum. Somebody delivered it, in the snare drum delivery truck. Somebody: reads the *Wall Street Journal*; vacuums the living room rug; measures the speed of neutrinos; packs the Orchid Fountain fireworks—thousands a day—into cartons destined for industrial shipping containers destined for shipping to America.

I was writing a poem, and I was working hard on that poem, with a hopeful energy. And even so, somebody else was laving salve—you need that layer, before the gentle layering of the gauze—on the terrible vinyl-like shine of a leg in the burn ward. An oily salve, intended to ease and heal the leg of a woman who won't be going back to *her* work, whatever it is, for a number of painful weeks.

. . .

Entire civilizations die. Genocide does that, of course, but so do changing weather patterns, or political unrest, or . . . any number of factors. (Those things can be as slippery to measure as neutrinos.) The Inca, the Aztecs: good-bye. (America might want to remember there's history here to learn from.)

On a smaller level, whole cities can die. Colorado copper mining communities, Kansas cattle trail communities: boom towns, overnight emptied of boom.

On the one-person level, what could be more impressively resplendent than a pharaoh's bon voyage? Look at those pyramids, the size of a mother ship waiting for its chosen Earthling to settle into his gold-and-lapis acceleration couch, for the starward journey. All four of his symbolic organs folded into preservative urns with god-headed stoppers. And all of his servants, sculpted as clay *shawabti* figures, six inches or so in height, each with the toothpick-size toy tool of his trade—a hoe, a fowling net, a papyrus scroll—to travel with him to the afterlife, and continue eternally laboring there.

We might want to remember that whenever a pharaoh extends the gilded flail-and-rod of god-on-Earth authority, somebody else is pausing, hoe in hand, in the field, to stretch out the muscle-crunch in his back. Somebody lashes him—that's a job too. Somebody hangs the rows of tinsel in the department store window displays at Christmas. Somebody oversees the membership of an international video game in which you choose the ghost you'll become one day, and play to accumulate reincarnation points. Somebody: porn. Somebody: genome splicing. Somebody: a poem, with a hopeful energy. Eight-year-olds worked fourteen-hour days in London's manufactories—dimly lit, unheated—and some of them, afterward, were twisted for the rest of their lives, like wax that had been softened and idly mangled, deformed by the spaces they needed to crawl inside while cleaning the machines.

In spring, Gillawney shows up on our block in his rattling flatbed, and calls out his services for mowing. In winter: shoveling snow, four feet of hard-packed stormfall some weeks, house after house. He has a buoyant, raffish air. But he'll also freely tell you about his ingrate son with the two outstanding warrants, about his wife and her drinking (and so, he claims, her walloping away at him), about the lump in his stomach but no insurance. In autumn: raking up the yellow and umber piles under the trees.

Who knows what, from inside of himself, he burns away with those leaves?

. . .

Somebody is N_____ and he's my friend. He has a disposition that leans, when given free rein, toward the mirthful. He has a curious mind, a benevolent heart. Still, his father: is dying of one of the uglier cancers that refuses to be carpet-bombed into submission. His mother: dementia. His PTSD from the explosive hills of Afghanistan: requires medication that, on bad days, muffles exactly the "curious mind" and "benevolent heart" of his better self. And on worse days: the VA won't renew his prescription.

His job is sculpting teeth for dental labs, *hand* sculpting teeth, the old school way, but digital-computerized zap-zap does it quicker and cheaper, and his once full-time employment has dwindled considerably. Soon it will be as vanished as a nineteenth century copper mining town, although his rent will still be due monthly.

When I think of my friends as a general unit . . . they aren't squirming through city sewers on their bellies to hose away clumps of solidified shit; but they sure aren't busy overseeing the lackeys who, in turn, oversee their million-dollar racing ponies, regatta yachts, and corporate spreadsheets. Magnates. My friends aren't magnates.

My friends . . . they're maybe a bit like you. Good people, facing adversity, in the you-range. Sometimes I see them as *shawabti* figures of baked clay, getting out of their tiny, baked clay beds in the morning. Wearing their dime-diameter crowns of thorns. Heading into their postage-stamp fires.

PANTHEON

In Mecca before Muhammad, pilgrims worshiped in a temple that had a statue of a different god for every day of the year.

—Neil MacGregor

Amazing. In that cosmos, how exactingly divisible
could faith be? Light: perhaps a separate god
for every color thinly banded along the spectrum?
Every blood cell? Dendrite? Breath?
The god of matter. The god of anti-matter. Today
the news is Carly tried to lift T up from the bed
in ICU, and the skin of T's right hand came off
in Carly's own hand "like an oily film." So much
for the vaunted wonders of chemotherapy.
Is there birdsong, is there sun as richly laid
as pats of butter on our cutlery, that somehow
manage to counterbalance such horror
and grief? The god of blatting traffic.
The god of the cookbook shelved in our kitchen.
Maybe every online pixel has its tutelary guardian.
I call on the god of today
to care, to deputize the fluttering dominions
of subsidiary gods: the one for ICU;
the one for the space where the air of the room
and the bloody mess of T's hand touch
without any barrier intervening. As for the sun
and the cutlery: they surely have their deities too.
How manifold does our prayer need to be?

So many reasons for gratitude, god of the bright dawn,
god of the blossoming taste buds. Yes, and so many
reasons to fear and beseech protection, o lord
of the high speed chase, of the Amber Alert, of EMS.
Tonight my wife is going to make her justly famous
mango meatloaf. At the moment
she's out in the birdsong and the traffic,
on her daily morning walk.
The god of a step. The god of the next step.

FIFTEEN

The first erotic movie?—in 1894,
not even two weeks from Edison's launch
of the first kinetograph parlor, one could, elsewhere,
view *Deloria in the Passion Dance*.
The first magazine advertisement to lure us

with sex?—in 1911, Woodbury's Facial Soap
transitioned from simply featuring a picture of its product
to the image of a hugging, affectionate couple,
plus this: *A Skin You Love to Touch*.
"In eight years, sales rose 1,000 percent."
Despite the serpent

and God, the Original Story is really
about the fig leaves, isn't it? Isn't that
what evolution demands of our focus? Today
I'm looking (circumspectly) at two sweetly clumsy
fifteen-year-olds shyly, proudly,
and clearly without rehearsal
of this tentative adventure,
step with a kind of coltish prancing
from the sidewalk into the garden part of the park,
in search of privacy
for something so uniquely outside of time, it's as if

they're inventing all of this,
you never existed, I never existed,
as if they're inventing the googoo eyes

and the pull on the heart toward dewy consummation,
inventing the wheel, inventing the taming of fire,
agriculture, pottery, the hafted spear,
as if the sun has never before
revealed the tree in this garden

like a key about to wind up the world.

UNWARRANTED EXPECTATIONS

That because the stars are a combination,
the sky is a code we can crack. (We
can't.) Because the night sky dresses up
in regalia for us, it cares.
(It doesn't.) Because her face (or his face)
in the river is [X], it will always be [X].
(It won't; and neither will the river.)
What did Lewis and Clark expect,
in naming a river they discovered Philanthropy River?
What aspirational dreamscape did they envision
nobly rising along its banks?
(In less than a generation, passersby
renamed it Stinking Water.)
Why are we always chumps for the game
where we topple a come-on stack
of milk bottles with a ball, and win
a love? (The carnival packs up overnight
and the love comes apart in a single washing.)
Still, there's beauty—a resilient, elliptical
beauty—in the way we line up hopeful
every time. It's true, if we chip away
all of the wood of a tree, what's left is *not*
a pure column of sun. And yet if we swivel
our expectation 180 degrees, a mound
of wood chips is its own reward. It's complicated,
here in the world. They force us out of the womb
—and then expect us to be happy.

UFOLOGY [*noun,* "the study of UFOs"]

It would be my prostate surgery
that let me see the thinness that exists

between the worlds—as thin,
perhaps, as the oxygenating wall of a red blood cell;

as thin as the breath between a god and a human being
that worked the bellows inside the lungs

of Jesus, for instance, or Hercules.
The stent that drained the serums from my bladder

into the clinical air of the operating room
seemed as astounding to me as one of those wormholes

science fiction novelists are always suggesting
might connect two galaxies

in a single pulse of starflash. Christopher told me
that, when he was writing a poem inside a café

on Fifth Avenue once, he looked up, through the window
to the street, and saw Dev standing in a mix of people

waiting for a bus. *Dev!*—"with that smile of his"—
and so Chris waved and stood to walk on out

with a hug: but then of course Dev disappeared,
he wasn't there because he's dead. Or

he was there, *was there,* but on a farther
and unhuggable plane of existence. Then Chris wept;

which, as you know, is a way
of briefly turning the body

inside out. They know this in medical school,
but use a different language. Something keeps

our mind and our epidermis functioning
in sync, although they really *are* two galaxies

with separate legislative understandings of the universe.
In Shakespeare's time, the Church helped ease the weight

of Lent's restrictions by categorizing chicken as "fish,"
and why not?—every solid,

including ourselves, is busy redoing its chemistry
(we can eavesdrop on uranium's famous

buzzy transformation). Just for sleep
and waking, we all require dual citizenship. And where

did I go to, how far did I travel, when
the anesthesiologist cleared the runway? All I know

is: when my wife and I first entered the clinic
and saw the lobby signage, I misread the "r"

of *urology:* "f"; but no, I wasn't there for a symposium
on the saucer people. I was there

for another kind of unidentified flying.

THE GOLDEN-CHEEKED WARBLER BREEDS ONLY WITHIN THE STATE OF TEXAS.

—caption on a post card

    It seems an unbelievably artificial containment, for so natural and explosive an activity. "This volcano erupted and darkened the sky for blocks in the 65257 zip code." "Meteors fall with regularity, creating fuming craters, in the parking lot down by the water slide." Still, who am I to argue the text of a post card?

    When I look back at my high school years, they sometimes seem like little more than great sap-driven attempts to get the breeding going, always spoiled by being in the wrong room, at the wrong time.

    We're all warblers, in our individual ways. Last night on my neighborhood walk I stopped before a house where, deep within, a couple—they look so ordinary, sitting on their porch in the afternoons—were going at it, whatever "it" was, on a level way past decibel-count. Breeding, maybe. That's one guess. Or maybe love had closed down for the night, and the meteors were falling.

THIS PATTERN

Election time, and the lawn signs
here on Echo Street overshadow
the flowers. Inevitably, the houses of boosters
of Candidate A and those of Candidate Z
are directly across the street from each other,
which makes the famous annual block party
. . . awkward. Or maybe "awkward" becomes insufficient
once EMS needs to be called, and the cops.

. . .

As for my friends the couple
whose only shared activity lately is talking about
*un*coupling . . . one day one says "Look,
we're smart, we can make this relationship work"
and the other one says "Oh right, you make it sound
so fucking easy" and then they trade those looks

a novelist might call "withering,"
you know: the "stinkeye," the "evil eye"
we were giving each other before
there was language, before the species
solidified its signature DNA.
It turns out money and sex are polarizing

and family and friends and career and location
and foods and religion

and what-movie-to-watch and where-to-shop
and politics

are polarizing.

. . .

Some scientists are imagining a telescope
with a thirty-foot-diameter liquid lens
we can build on the moon.
On the moon! The cost would be [joke coming up]
astronomical; and we're still short
of the supertechno-ability required; but
once it exists we can look at the stars

so far away in time, they'd be (they'd give forth)
what cosmologists call "first light"
—the original radiation of the original stars
created by the Big Bang,
in the moment (not that "moments" existed)
when Nothing and Something argued for control,
for domination . . .
                              and so established this binary pattern
of adversarial thinking
we live by today.

. . .

Eventually
the election signs get pulled away,
and the front lawn flowers—just look at them!—

are visible again,
emerged as if from an eclipse.
I've often watched how here on Echo Street

the trees on both sides
—long-established bearers of voluptuous,
green boughs—lean, at their highest,
toward the center of the street,
and meet there, blending indistinguishably,

and make a single canopy,
and make it look to our human stares
as if it were fucking easy.

THE SONG OF THE PRACTICAL

Increasingly, those water lilies of Claude Monet's
became unbodied—were yolk, and mist, and cream
and primal amniotic murk, a swirly haze
of rapturous seeing: "a dream
of infinity," one critic accurately said.
But even a dream is rooted
in the physical—in a brain, in a head
that's also suited
for actuarial tables, for the vision
of lawyers, accountants, hatchet CEOs.
My wife and I once saw a magician
rise from the stage and—who knows
how?—float over the wide-eyed audience,
lighter than meringue, without
mirrors or wires or smoke, a sense-
confounding moment, a mahout
without an elephant beneath. And still,
although the ushers sat us
directly below a seeming miracle,
we *knew* that it required apparatus,
strategic planning, expense—there had to be
attention paid to the practical, the daily grind,
the union wages, the catering truck, the heavy
shlepping of roadies—behind
that moment of weightless wonder. Monet
"once summoned the local barber to cut his hair"
while he painted, while he continued his day
of communing with spirit and cosmos and air.

LANDSCAPE WITH PEACH TREES

I'm speaking of small sadnesses. So many,
and so intimate. A dozen will cram in the ghetto of one
ovarian cyst. I've seen a sadness
fit in the shadow cast by a single impasto stroke of paint
in Van Gogh's *Peach Blossom in the Crau*.
In this picture it's midday.
The sky is a school of many blue dazzles.
The road is so long, and the bushes so mossily cool
—they don't provide much shade,
but enough for this tramp. I won't go into why
and how his life is more torn than even his coat.
Just take my word for it. And that coat . . .!
He'll curl in the shade, the fragrance of peach tree
is his quilt. He'll sleep,
he'll sleep there till you find him,
till you stumble on him. You turn him over
into the light
and startle, seeing
his face is your own.

"TO CURE THE TOOTH-ACH, TAKE A NEW NAIL, AND MAKE THE GUM BLEED WITH IT, AND THEN DRIVE IT INTO AN OAK."

—John Aubrey (circa 1680)

Because Stewie's girlfriend Dangergirl
is in lockdown tonight, in lockdown in a straitjacket
so her self-cut arms can hug her chest
like a crest—*two lengths of ladder rungs
crossed over a pale field of double mastectomy*—
I'm including in this stanza the common roofing nail
she used, and that she photographed and posted
in her "cry for help" which echoed all day
in the cyberair of the Web until her parents erased it;
and even though Stewie and Danger don't know
Wendell and how drink has done to his memory what chemo
did to his hair, I'm including the nail for him

as well; and for Antoine and Dora, you can see divorce
upon their faces like the cracks that start
to thread across old wall paint; and the mothers
picking through the mounded bodies in that ditch
in that crazily genocidal nation in the news, until
each one has found her own death-hardened child and laid it out
on its back in the day's insulting sunshine;
and for Eddie, even—just Eddie, and his loneliness
we've been hearing about blahblah blahblah for years:
it's a real enough two tons of emotional hurt to *him*.
For every one of them: the nail. Let it absorb some of the coppery
taste of their pain. And now because I've always been fascinated

by sympathetic magic—the dug-up tuber that reverses
male impotency, because of its shape; the ruby
(precious, blood-red, and mineral-hard) that serves to guard
the hymen—I must pile up such completely and intentionally
extraneous recountings as, say, those of the intrepid
nineteenth-century balloonists who first realized
an aerial map of the country could be made by night,
acoustically (one dog-bark meant "a lonely, isolated farm";
a chorus of barking, "villages or railheads"; and silence itself
"spoke eloquently of the great open prairies"), while daylight
revealed that insects—lacewings, ladybirds, butterflies—
rise "to about nine thousand feet," a living, graceful

zoetrope around the explorers' wicker encasement. So
many adventures!—in 1979, two doughty cetologists who
were studying a pair of breeding gray whales ventured a little
too close: the female swam beneath their "small
inflatable research craft," and, at that craft-and-coochie
alignment-moment, the male began to hammer his impressive
penis into her, and "we were used as a diaphragm." Wonder
webs our psyche like the lace inside a tangerine.
And the purpose of this oak-thick mess of exempla I've been
listing above? . . . well, somewhere in the hodgepodge of it all
I've driven a nail; and with it I'm burying
its consignment of torments: Dangergirl's;
Wendell's; Dora's; Eddie's; all those mothers'; even yours.

MEDIATION POEM

This is why Hercules crushes the throat of the bull
until it feels like oatmeal stuffed in a velvet sleeve
beneath his fingers. This is why Icarus plummets,
dragging his great contrail of screams behind; and why
his father has to witness. Why Atalanta somehow survives
abandonment in infancy on the mountainside,
and grows to be a maiden who slays two centaurs
with an arrow in the hearts of their human halves.
Why Helen looks in the mirror and can't distinguish
her golden hair from the fires that eat up Troy.

So we don't need to hack a gateway in our breasts
and admit those enormities. Let Abraham
tie his son among the thorns, and let Delilah bear
her guilt among the dust of the fallen columns
—for us, so we don't need to take
the full, unmediated force of those adventures.

Why Han Solo, Princess Leia.
Why Harry Potter is a candelabrum of lightning
on the battlements, and somewhere a woman
enters the entire spectrum (fifty shades)
of gray and can never exit again.
Let Ahab, Madame Bovary
announce us to the world, and bring the world
to us—so that we can endure and continue.
Why Jesus. *Let* him. *We*
don't want to die for our sins.

The entire "we" of us—our "self"—relies
on mediation. As only two examples:
eardrum; lens of eye.
Imagine the ecstasy of the reed
in the harmonica, that amplifies
our breath into a soulfulness
they can hear even out on the street
a block up from the blues bar: it's an ecstasy
that would split us apart, if the reed
didn't serve as ambassador. Mars:
do you know what Mars would do to your lungs?
That's why we have the Curiosity rover.
When Natalie (street name Mixup)
owed the Devil's Dudes more money

than her family made in a year—or, failing the money,
a night of free blow jobs for all eight blood-oath members
and any invited friends—and, failing that,
the debt would be paid to a cloth-wrapped
ten-inch length of pipe—her parents

arranged to meet Teebo and Shorty in an alley
and said, with united, fumbling bravado (and expecting
their antagonists might then back off), "Okay,
do it to us." And, shrugging, not caring much
either way, so long as word got out
the goddam debt was paid, they did.

Mediation: Milton's daughters
feeling the waste of their flowering prime,

while simultaneously feeling the glory
as *Paradise Lost* is dictated to them,
on-fire word by word. In the language of marijuana,
a contact high.

At night the moon allows us
to stare at the light of the sun without going blind.

THE LIMITED TIME

*The first book reputed to have been printed
without any errors appeared only in 1750.*

—Adrian Johns

In the story as I heard it, that advisor of tyrants,
Machiavelli, adamantly refused to renounce the devil
on his deathbed. "Father, where I'm going,"
he said to the priest, "I can't afford to make enemies."
An admirable show of self-assessment (and
-acceptance), shit stains, warts and all.
The rest of us?—our flaws are always tapping
at the brain's back door to be admitted:
"Hey, don't leave for your honeymoon tonight
[or father's funeral, or meeting with the press, etc.]
without us." In that, we have the tiny, frequent shames
my friends know, who believe (against all evidence and logic)
that the path of evolution should be ethical as well;
yet here they all are, undeniably ambitionmongers,
spitters on the luck of others, silent destroyers
of trust . . . like anybody else, as cankered in their spirit
as the moon is on its face. And yes: my father's
funeral *is* an apt example: there I was,
my tongue a thick, caked work boot
kicking the mourner's *kaddish* around in my mouth.
The woe was honest, strong; my heart, though,
had been offered to some love-angst
of that current tortured, after-the-divorce time in my life;

its tithe of me was therefore withheld
from the elegiac grieving at his service
—and I live, still, with the guilt of this. My father,
of course, was perfect by then: a newly polished
doll of death, untouchably beyond
the many messy and partisan tugs of human dailiness.
And what of the extremes, the "incorruptibles"?—Saint Isidore,
for instance, whose cadaver, forty years from the year
of its burial, was disinterred "and found to be without any
sign of decay, but a sweet and ravishing odour emanated forth";
in 1969, *800 years* from the year of its burial, it was
"darkened, rigid, but perfect," displayed in Madrid
for thousands of the faithful there. Miraculous!
Another way of saying that: "unnatural."
Admit it: we don't have a hope of being (or would *want*
to be) a thing so inhumanly out
of the bounds of the laws of thermodynamics; all of our wants
and pleasures, all of the secret dreamydreams we feed on
with such satisfaction . . . these would be discredited. Instead,
when I think of my auntie Hannah's dying this last week
—my father's sister, now beside him—it's her quirks,
which lasted even through the lung-pain and the blood-pain,
that I'm fondest of . . . her clichés, and her ditziness . . .
they please me in the way the first few typos that I saw
in published poems of mine seemed dire then, but wholly
charming now, and part of the human fabric: *rabbi*
changed to *rabbit*; *barns* to *bras*. Look,
we're as good as it gets, in the limited time we're given.
My aunt was eighty-nine. Three centuries,
it took for the book to be flawless.

WINE / OK / FLOWERS

Of course it's difficult for them
—the hero and villain in a time travel novel—
attempting to carry something against
the "natural" "direction" of time.
Just standing still
on the transporter's central disc,
they pant as if in cardiovascular extremity.
"To carry something"—even a guppy, a feather,
even a thumbtack, even what any carpenter calls
an ordinary coating of sawdust . . . trying to carry these trifles
forward or backward is like crossing over
one of those high-speed-chase strips
the police throw down: what the physicists
in those novels call the "continuum" of time "flow"
is its own police, and redoes human circumstance
as needed, to keep its "stream" in appropriate
chronological order. And yet I refuse
to privilege the characters in those books;
it's tough for *all* of us, since any minute leading
into the next is also travel
over time—eight hours' sleep has often
reconfigured lives—and keeping faithfulness intact,
and our hopes, our diligence, our dear unduplicatable
selves unchanged
from day to day—beyond mutation,
uncontaminated—is one of our most arduous
humdinger labors. 90% of most wine
can't transport itself across two years

without declining chemically into another,
lesser self. Time travel is landmined
with complexities. "The American 'OK' sign
—thumb and forefinger forming a circle—[meant]
an obscenity in ancient Greece."—John Mann.
"Bees flown from France to New York
went searching for nectar in Paris time, and
discovered that the flowers in the Big Apple
had yet to open."—*Fortean Times*.
Sometimes if I'm awake before my wife,
I'll watch her stir from sleep
in a nuanced, yawny progression, slowly widening
the invisible caul of dreamself
that still clings to her; I impatiently wait
in the Time Society Greeting Pavilion
to see that she's made the mystery journey
glitchlessly. And me?—when I wake, if I have the leisure,
I linger for a moment . . . *yesterday was* A *and* Y;
today I intend to do B *and* Z . . . connecting these across the divide,
getting my bees and nectar in order.

VARIOUS METRICS

First there was the Era of Sex-
Before-There-Were-Sex-Robots. Now,
the Era of Beckoning Digisex
(already there's a robot that
[a robot "who"?] self-lubricates).
Soon, the Era of Bio-Android Life.
In fact, we live in the Era-of-Eras-
Supplanting-Earlier-Eras-Too-Quickly-To-Monitor.
My grandmother's life began in Kitty Hawk
and ended in Sputnik. That's a metric
so outdated now—so abacus slow,
so hieroglyphics slow—it may as well
be the minutes that crawled past on their knees
as she sat at the back of the kitchen
plucking the chicken free of its feathers,
one by one, or lacing up her boots
with the use of a buttonhook, in the Era of Buttonhooks,
one by one, one by one.

. . .

And then my grandmother died and then
my mother died and then the radio died
and was reborn (amen!) as the television, and then,
by which I mean now, I asked my wife to look up
the definition of "era" on the internet. These units
change so swiftly that they *don't* change,
they're the textures of a single continuous flow.

We use "era" so casually, as I've been doing
—the era of crewcuts, of Betamax, of rap—
and yet originally it was long,
was *long*, "the era from the founding of Rome
to its fall," "the Christian era," etc.
How long is a mountain?—a minute,
in the terms of the Era of Light.

. . .

    Of the Wright brothers' flight in December 1903 at
    Kitty Hawk, North Carolina, the world's first true
    airplane flight: it "lasted just twelve seconds and
       was shorter than the wingspan of a modern jumbo jet"
(Bill Bryson).

The length of that journey, 120 feet, could be a metric
for the idea of technological advance,
a unit I hereby term a "wright." Let's say
from naked eye, to Galileo's lenses, to
a rocket-blasted, assemble-the-pieces-in-space,
impossible-but-somehow-real
amazingness is [so many] wrights. So many forward leaps!
But some things *don't* evolve; the human things, as opposed
to the things that humans think up. When my friend
S. B. first heard about the shooting in Texas
    [*which one?*—this most recent one, where the 18-year-old
    brought his AR-15-style semi-automatic rifle
      into the elementary school in Uvalde and slaughtered
    nineteen children—*ten-year-olds*—after earlier

>   shooting his grandmother in the face, here
>   in the American Era of Wrongness]
she fell to her knees "and then I curled up
into the fetal position, Albert, and just lay there
as if I'd been hit by a truck." We've seen that position
repeatedly through time, in the sacrificial victims
arranged that way on mountain tops
for a deity's appeasement, in the graves of one millennium
after another. It never changes,
somehow, even as the synth-skin on the robo-dolls
gets creamier and more responsive to fondling
every year. "I just lay there, completely unfeeling."
How many wrights from a rock to a rifle?
How many things can go wrong in a day?

. . .

Russia launched Sputnik ("fellow earth traveler")
in 1957, and a little over three years later
Yuri Gagarin became the first person in space,
in the spaceship *Vostok*. By now, there's a congested
LA freeway or an Autobahn of traffic
spinning in orbit. Such a busy sky!—above

my grandma Nettie's grave. She was buried in 1961
and still serves, under her grassy mound, as a stopped clock
from a different kind of time: a time

not demarcated by change. In her life before America,
laundry was done in a huge communal cauldron

over a fire, stirred with what were basically oars.
A widow, she lived with us, this quiet, Yiddish-speaking woman
no taller than many twelve-year-olds,
and our 1950s washer-dryer (avocado green)
was as astonishing to her as "cybernetics"
or "supersonic" or "Big Bang" or "atomic powered"
would have been—had there been Yiddish words.
As a child, I almost never spoke to her,

but I'd love (too late) to talk with her now,
to hear about how the rabbi was paid in dumplings and eggs,
and what it was like to be seventeen
and sighing under that village moon, and if
she remembered the stink of her sisters loosing their bowels
when the Cossacks galloped into the main street
looking for Jew-filth to rape. I'd ask her that,
I'd ask her how many things could go wrong
in a day back then, I'd ask her to sing
and I'd ask her what it was like to smile contentedly
in the arms of the man I'm named after.
But if you want to talk with her now,

it isn't in Yiddish, or the small English she learned.
You have to talk with the grass,
which she's become. And the grass doesn't care
about our many tongues—our babble.
No, it speaks the language "Always"
—a soliloquy it began at the start
of the Era of Forever.

FOREVER HALF-DONE

When I think of Selena the Seven-Year-Old Wonder
I think of Pompeii. It goes like this: onstage
she juggles three live chickens (drugged; but still, impressive),
sings a medley of patriotic tunes while deftly committing
a jitterbuggish hopscotch through a stage-wide map
of the forty-eight states, then wows 'em with a wrap-up where,
blindfolded, she ticks off the contents of that night's
portliest audience member's purse or pocket. Offstage

she's a seven-year-old in a glittered and battered world
of tasseled burleyque hoofers and heehaw vaudeville clowns
—she'll never be eight, then nine, she'll be this
strangely precocious seven for eighty more years, for
three confounded husbands and uncountable though equally
confounded casual beaus. She's one time,
carried through the rest of time, the rare case
of a personality sidestepped out of change. And so reminding me

of the way the bread was found half-done—forever
half-done—on the baker's wooden oven-spade,
its dough braid more like stone by now; the way
the change in payment for a goblet of wine was still there
on the counter top, a stuck gear, while the world
of finance continued, elsewhere, fluttering
and destroying; the way, mid-flight, the ash-stunned bird dropped
like a stone bird, at the feet of people who

also dropped, from the gas and the ash, mid-everything:
we've uncovered them in a rictus of aborted human doing
from love through terror. Many are frozen in panic,
fleeing, of course, but look: this girl, a "maiden"
she'd have once been called, is drooped across
the tile ledge of a window-square so jarringly at peace
with her unentered future, she becomes more painful
to our looking than the frantic ones. This poem,

. . .

I see, is come to be an elegy for anything inside us
that's a stalled clock; and for many of my friends
that means an early dream—say,
"ribbon-winning violin concertist"—pickled whole, in its aglow,
untested, homuncular skin, as startling as that row
of bottled fetuses at the Museum of Science and Industry
I viewed as a child: all those increasingly-detailed paisleys
bobbled against their lids. Okay, so this is a poem,

I admit it now, about my student Shelly Hiebert, twenty-two,
in a tin can of a car, in that deceitful winter half-light,
out of Newton, Kansas, into the twists surrounding
Newton, Kansas, on ice, with the ribboned Christmas packages
loosely heaped in the trunk, with fifty-eight actuarial and
demographic years still in her future, with the tree
in her future, the tree just minutes away in a ballet
of fate and velocity. The stone bread

. . .

spirals forth its thread of stone steam: ancient;
ancient and new. Shelly Hiebert will always be twenty-two.

CAPPED

That this dainty bone
—the leg bone of a mouse,
precision-shaped as only a zillion years
of evolution will, and angled up
from the pellet of owl dung as startlingly
as Excalibur angled out of its stone—
astonishes us in coming across it
is natural enough: we know the long, dark
alimentary journey it's undergone, and yet
retained its shape, its ivory gleam here
in the daylight; and we start to list

the other intact remains we've seen or heard of:
a tentacle, roundeled with its suckers, regurgitated
out of a shark; a beetle
one friend found one morning—glistening
yet, like a countess's ring
of jade and garnet—riding a finger-length of scat
in the corner litter box. If these are enough

to astonish us—these objects remaining impeccably
complete after traveling the distance of a digestive tract—
no wonder senses wobble over some of the detail
—down to a single vein in a leaf, or a vein
that scraggles an eyelid—still compellingly vivid over travel
measurable in millennia:

the sacrificial victims who were bound in rope
and consigned to a bog: capped-over
by that preservative water
holding them safe from the usual undoings,
so that the intaglio sprig of tiny lines
—of crowsfeet—subtly emphasizing a woman's eyes
is perfectly legible still; as is

the residue of leaves and fruit in the stomach
of this *Darwinius masillae*, a fossil
("nearly twenty-three inches from nose to tip of tail,"
an elegant comet-arc of bone) that they've
unearthed fastidiously from 47 million years ago
when it was capped by the crust of the planet
as effectively as a Mason jar caps figs; as is

the fabled population of Pompeii, taken out
of its capping of hardened ash, some bodies
so whole, so particular, we can read their stories
—the mother, for instance, attempting to shelter
her child under herself—in a startling eloquence
of wrinkle and gnarl, of fanned-out hands,
that hasn't been diminished by time; as is
the tract of meadow flowers (their petals
infant's-fingernail-sized) that became
the fossils of flowers under a cap of ash and lava
and still look, if we squint the right way, as if
they might wave in a meadow breeze. And so

I need to consider S_____: her jail tatts,

their pinprick cloudy outlines, one
for every kid that Social Services removed by force
from her arms, and one for the hustling mac
who broke her and taught her "the life," and one
for every bullet hole in the side of the BMW
she somehow crawled-on-all-fours from
alive; oh, and one for the shank scar
that some capable jailhouse artiste was inspired to use
as the centerpoint of a lavishly unfurled tattoo rose.
And you'd be right in thinking she's good

at faking showcased merriment and ease (or thinking faking
is the very air she breathes) but that even
her laughter and her sexual allure are glints
on hardness, on a body—on a life—that's become,
of necessity, all carapace. Was she open, ever,
to communing with the stars
in their grandeur and solitude,
that sky-show so more vast than any receiving system
our brain has; did the adventure of being alive here,
floating wonder-eyed inside
the nervous system of infinity
ever have her feeling at one with the luckier
lives of some of my friends?
That, I can't answer. But I do know

she was bound in rope, metaphorically,
and sacrificed to the difficult gods of this world;
and thrown into the bog of it,
down to its bottom: and then

capped over by a toughened desensitized surface;
and is waiting to be excavated,
waiting to be resurrected—*if* that ever happens—
into the light of daily ongoingness:
each moth-wing eyelid and cuticle
as perfect, still, as when her mother
kissed them just seconds after her birth.

MY LIFE AMONG THE AFTERLIVES

1.

Do we need another poem

about them? No.
Yes, I meant yes, we do,

we do so that we'll have written about the ones
that wheedle plaintively on the lawn at night,
all night, until their need for recognition is appeased
with a ruby bulbette of hen blood
set in a hollowed nutshell in the grass;

the ones who take up comfy residence
in mannequins in the trendier boutiques,
and then the lushly painted plaster lips
are *their* lips, and the saris or the lookee-lookee
miniskirts are baskets where *their* longing is kept
among us, still, between generic plaster thighs;

the prankster ones that rearrange [the prankster ones *who* rearrange?]
the haunted pub's ranked rows of ale tankards
overnight, when the mopped-up premises are vacant; the warrior
ones, on horses similarly spectral; the nunnery ones;
the ones the size of a loaf of bread, who were released
from out of a corpse the size of a loaf of bread; and even Casper,
the "friendly" one . . . who'd ever have guessed that one of the shades
would one day be a copyrighted property? We need

to write about them—yes. To latch them here,
to stop them from their final disappearing,

or the ghosts will turn into whatever ghosts
turn into that pass, in their own way, for ghosts.

2.

Golf is Scottish in origin

as is bogey, "an old Scottish term for a ghost or spirit."
And so bogey became the term for a notional "best score"
on a given hole; the idea was you were scoring
"against a hypothetical bogey man." Now let me

get this straight: my mother,
who didn't sleep all night so she could check
on her feverish son at half-hour intervals…
my father, who worked twelve-hour days so
(this is reductive in its symbology, but no less true)
his son could go to college…*they*

have never for a second drifted like recognizable mist
across my vision (or my sister's); never once,
a posthumous dew or whisper or rattling attic curtain-pull,

but every goddam *golfer* gets to have a phantom companion?

. . .

My mother, however, lingers in my imagination.
She always dreamed of becoming—but never did—
an artist . . . sketching the heads of women (with au courant bobbed hairdos)
staring toward the sketchpad margin into a future life
more glamorous than her own. And so I sometimes imagine her
that career . . . a studio, a palette, an easel.
Maybe in that existence her sister Regina *doesn't* die
of a cancer cratering her brain. . . .
A ghost unnaturally clings to its past, and yet this
artist-Fannie-Goldbarth functions as an anti-ghost:
she's real;
but by the standards of a past that never existed.

3.

The ones who greeted Odysseus
on his there-and-back trip to the Underworld
—the heroes of old. Their skin was as cold
to his fingers as a mountain stream
and, like the stream, they held to their approximate shape
even as currents ran through them.

The ones on the ski slope,
tethered by a molecular chain of zero degrees
to the site of the accident. Visitors
report seeing, or almost seeing, what looks
like a bridal veil fluttering behind the falling snow.

The college (or pro team) mascot ones: the dead
come back as outsized, clumsily capering
faux-rhinos, -chickens, -wolverines.

The ones who sing a sad air in a minor key
inside the walls of a hardware store
(for sale) that once, in the copper mining
heyday of this Montana town, was a thriving bordello.
The ones who sing a deeply melancholy
basso profundo melody somewhere
in the played-out walls
of the nearby mine (abandoned).

They all have this in common (whether love; or revenge;
or a message to deliver):
unfinished business

here, in the corporeal realm;
and only its completion will unlock them
from their ectoplasmic, bleary
indeterminacy.

. . .

But all of that assumes
that ghosts are exterior. I think that they're
—if anything—our memories
(either individual memories, or cultural)
that we give wigs,
toupees, long dresses that visually warble
in even the stillest air, chains, doublets, sabers, keening laments,

and prop them up, and send them on their way,
when really they're not themselves

but us
—the way that a funeral
isn't for the dead,
but the living.

4.

In Sean Russell's fantasy trilogy *The Swans' War*,
we meet Cyndll, a wandering "story finder," whose task
is to travel the outlands with his especially sensitized
psychic antenna tuned to what remains
of ancient stories . . . gnarled under the roots,
marbled into the sediment, gritting the wind. . . .

"We are alive, though briefly. Then we are memory,
for the lives of those who knew us. And then
we are story—stor[ies] last longest of all. . . . They
echo in the places where they were told
or where they were lived." And

me? I have my psychic antenna for stories
too. Just last week Kaylie told me she didn't know
which one of the two was the daddy, and she was going
to try to swab Bodette's cheek in his sleep
for a home paternity test kit. Taylor
or Bodette . . . two futures tremulously existing

in potential, one on the wavery chemical tip of becoming
actualized, and one about to enter the borderless land
of Wasn't/Won't-Be . . . where the ghosts conduct their business
on either side of the present tense.

The next time you're in a motel for the night,
I suggest that you set your ear against the mattress
and the pillow with something of Cyndll's
persistent quest for the remnants of narrative

and then brace yourself.

5.

Sometimes when you remove your hat
from your head, for a moment
the head remembers the hat.

The ones that dance in a ring
where two roads cross, and so eddy the moonlit air.
The stillbirth ones. The ones that play
the creak and slam and whooshing of a house at night
like symphonists—woodwinds, tubas, tambourines.
So many. As many as we are.
Yes, but for now I want to consider my mother

walking through the hill land in the early morning,
until she finds the perfect vista and there sets up
the easel I've imagined for her,

unpacking her brushes, paints, ceramic mixing trays.
For a while—necessarily long—she simply stares
along this pearly-gray and verdant distance,
as the nearest details soften
in their travel toward the horizon line,
the green become more gray, and then the gray
become more hazy, and finally everything
given away to air.

SMEARS AND SHIMMERS

Whoever he was, he left his glasses sitting
on the counter at Theresa's Diner; one side,
held together with about three inches of scrunched-up tape;
one lens, smeared with lipstick still in the partial shape
of a woman's lips. That's all we know. The life
that we surmise is based on this one relic,
this mysterious clue—the way we read
entire civilizations into a few ceramic fragments
left in the earth. Who were their gods? How did they love?
What word would have been on that woman's lips?

. . .

In Grant Wood's sketch for *The Birthplace of Herbert Hoover*,
a tree in the yard casts a shadow that looks
like an egg whisk. Chickens have their shadows,
also laundry on the line: small gray-tone accent marks.
A man points at the house; so does his shadow,
like some stylized international sign for "point."
And in the round of a stream, a thin reflected length
of the house is floating upside-down. If everything
else, everything *real*, in this sketch were erased . . . how much
would we know of the world from just its smears and shimmers?

. . .

Whoever he was, he wrote a poem called "Smears
and Shimmers." That's all we know. It isn't much

to go on: if we have the feet of an ancient statue,
how do we picture the body they held up? Still,
we can try. It's why we need to make the marks we leave
be marks we can be proud of. Someone read that poem,
some woman or man, and left a crease,
or finger smudge, or shadow on the page.
It's here if you look. A shadow is here if you look,
and it's pointing at something, whatever it is.

CLAY POTTERY SHARDS: *Pueblo Culture, Pecos*

How far can affinity kinship
be extended, and "cousin"
still be a viable term?

We know there's clay on Mars
and, if we credit those photographs
from the Curiosity rover, it's
the color of New Mexico clay.

A family resemblance.

. . .

On our last day in Santa Fe,
Tony gives Skyler and me, one each,
a pottery shard,
dusty and authentic, about two inches by one:
umber-tone, with what looks like a length
of black fretwork arcing across it.

"They would drill a hole, and wear it
as the pendant of a necklace."
Turning rubble to adornment.
And although they left no written language,
this—the urge to embellish themselves
with artifactual beauty—is something

that translates easily into a life
we understand. Even those science fiction adventures

I read at age fourteen...even on another planet . . .
another planet! . . . evil was fought;
and romances were kindled; and warriors,
priests, and great cosmopolitan beauties
exhibited decoration in ways that we could recognize,

as if their Martian god created,
like ours,
the first human beings from clay.

THE GOLDEN FLOWER OF DEEPEST TIME

Ten billion dollars—that's a lot

of recliner chairs, weed whackers, and quarter-pounders,
and my mind goes *wow!* in wonder along with yours
at that cost of the James Webb telescope NASA launched
last Saturday. As with you, it's the price
(let's get those zeroes lined up on parade: 10,000,000,000)
that grabs my fancy first, but really *everything*

about this outbound techno-eye is guaranteed
to jitter our astonishment. Gold-plated,
flower-shaped, its folded ("much like origami,"
say the press releases) twenty-one-foot mirror,
when at last unfurled, will be "the most sensitive,
largest mirror ever launched, or so far realistically conceived of";
then, protected by "a tennis court-size
sunshield that provides subzero shade," it will offer

our first glimpse of the faint light from . . . well,
pretty much from the birth of light,
13.7 billion years in the past. The way
the obstetrician or midwife
slaps your toosh to open your lungs to your life,
this astronomical marvel sharply startles our understanding
into the life of the cosmos, star by next star. So whatever

the vocabulary word might be that makes "amazing" inadequate
—whatever the next-intensifier word is—
that's what this is. Even so,

it feels so distant (not only in millions of miles,
but also in our planetarium-dome-of-a-skull's ability
to hold such ideas and numbers). . . . Give me

instead the chance to knock for luck
against the lumpy surface of the meteorite
Steve Arnold found in 2005 in an otherwise
unpretentious Kansas wheat field:
it's 1,430 pounds—a braille text
of extraterran travel, and it says
that some of the story of cosmic astoundingness
is tangible, is capturable
by a ten dollar throwaway camera from the Shop-&-Save:
astoundingness enough for my laboring noggin.
I'm no enemy of abstraction, but

if "God" is "out there" "somewhere" or even "everywhere,"
still, I'm looking right now at one of the morning glories
that my wife coaxed out of our garden's urban soil,
its petals a rich cream dabbed with tiny sprawls
of pinkish-purple something like the inner lip
of whelks I've seen; and surely this—although
no "burning bush"—is also a face of the divine.

And "Time": the orbits of our planets are rings,
like tree rings: saying a story
of how old the solar system is.
Still, Google *kalpa* (Sanskrit) and you'll see
how laughably flicker-brief even *that* story is.
Today, though, it's enough that I'm seventy-five

with the ophthalmologist and urologist appointments
on my calendar. It's *more* than enough.

"Death": somewhere
waaay over there, a tsunami, an earthquake, a genocide:
a thousand? four thousand? six million?
In the British-Sudanese war of 1898,
11,000 Sudanese died and 13,000 were wounded.
But that's so far back, those corpses may as well
have piled up, indeed, in the universe's original
appearance of light. It's not at all like the saffron light
of the afternoon when you looked out your window

and saw—and heard—your next-door neighbor's
eight-year-old bounce off the grill of a hit-and-run car,
and as you punched in 9-1-1
you could see a bone begin to slip out of its muscle
and hear, inside the purely animal moans,
the one word *momma*, again, again.

Two thousand and thirty-five: the number of words
that are introduced to the world in Shakespeare's plays.
One list begins with "abstemious" and "antipathy"
and stretches to "zany." (And then there were words
like "exsuffligate" too, that had a shorter shelf life.)
But tell me . . . some days, isn't
the pleasure dome and land mine lengths
of "love" sufficient?

Oh yes, "love" is out there. Fifty gazillion
poems from sappy to guruesque-sagacious,
fifty gazillion valentine cards, and songs, and
/ oh wait, excuse me a moment, right now

my wife is pulling into the carport
after some shopping, now she's getting out. What I know,
that you don't, are the hard-won battles [abstraction]
and fierce determinations [abstraction] that became the rungs
of her life for so long [abstraction]. But
if you were here alongside me, you would see [in specificity]
the light tangled up in her auburnish hair,
and a smile like the fulfillment of a binding contract
made between herself and herself, for happiness.

You may know of Lucy, over three million years old,
our famous hominid ancestor named by her two discoverers
after "Lucy in the Sky with Diamonds"
—over forty percent of her skeleton,
the baton bones and the jackstraws bones
and the ocarina bones and the butterfly bone, preserved
"miraculously . . . in the badlands of Hadar in Ethiopia."
And so she has an Ethiopian name as well, that I invoke
as my wife goes *tap* to her fob and the Kia locks with an oink:
Dinknesh,

"You are marvelous."
Now she's walking up to the porch with her bags
of gluten-free bread and framing supplies
as if it were an everyday occurrence, and not an example
of how Mystery and Revelation
are still at work in this ho-hum world.
It's as if she just landed here out of the sky.

HISTORY: SNAPSHOTS, 2

And Snow

—like us,
a paraphrase of water.

. . .

So much like a Renaissance figure of Death:
the old-time photographer under his black hood.

I suppose a photograph *is* (the way orgasm
is sometimes referred to as) a "little death,"

a flash (a flesh) that then immediately
becomes the past. My friends have seen a sonogram,

their child in her womb—so new, he floats
in her like an unhardened dollop of glass

her breath's still shaping, and his earbones
are only a dream of her body's own calcium. And yet

if being gilled is having history, he's already old
by tens of thousands of years. A clock requires just

two atoms—time is comparison.
Already he's a million atoms, furiously ticking.

THE SYSTEMS

Sleeping away from the primacy. Sleeping, you might say
slipping, together away from the first night's paradigmatic
passion-and-slumber. She looks across
their bed: he's dozing. He's a version
of someone she once loved, and he's connected
to that person by a continuous stream of versions
of himself. She sees now, anything

implies a system attached to it. A penny
glinting sharply on the noontime street implies
the entire sun. A fact implies its possibly being gossiped
through a secondary network. Nobody exists outside
of a context of other people. She
remembers two lines from a poem by Chu Ch'ing-Yü.
Some court ladies are walking the pavilion:

They want to talk of palace matters
But dare not, in front of the parrots.

HIGH NOON

From the office next door: a *typewriter,* here
in 2022? Well, no . . . but it *is* the tapshoe clattering
of a typewriter in the background
of a 1940s black-and-white movie
. . . and suddenly
the old, familiar fondness washes over me
for all of the disappearing:
the corner mailbox, sprocketed film. . . .
Nostalgia is like a shadow we cast
in one direction only:
backward. Some days it's surprising
it allows me to take even one step ahead.

. . .

"It all changes so *fast,*" Delanie complained,
as she held up her gleaming new miracle phone,
a sleek thing crammed with algorithmic magic:
"I *know* in a year it'll be outdated"
by another, sleeker, crammier device
(or maybe a digi-implant, smaller than a pea)
that unleashes some bunny hop or conga line
of supersonic pixelated streaminglingo
forming in front of her retina, telling her what
to think. "I already feel nostalgia for
this stupid thing," and she held it up again,
"nostalgia in embryo."

EVERYDAY VERSION

In the kitchen. Sprinkling fragrant pinches
of a recipe she's clipped: the clove,
the ginger, the nutmeg, folded in
routinely and routinely blended. This is our current

everyday version. For these, however, so long ago
it's mythic, we braved a voyage of tempests,
deadly lulls, sea serpents, dragons. These, we brought
in golden vases to the manger.

AFTER LAST NIGHT

is this day. I think everything would be that
simple—thoughtlessly sequential—if only
we could abandon ourselves to the wheel
of sun and moon entirely, without the neocortex
and its burdens: language; likening; inference.

Look at these huge museum displays—the reconstructed bodies
of creatures whose skeletons we could clamber
inside of like lighthouses . . . not one penny
of human confusion ever dropped through there. But
us?—we need our symbols, our continuous
self-reference. For instance, here: the bones
of two more, set up just as they were excavated, interjumbled
with one another: *"We don't know*
if they were copulating or locked together in battle."

ONE WEEK BEFORE THE DIVORCE IS FINAL

they start to laugh at something
they find mutually funny, laughing,
hating that they're laughing

and at night they sleep in separate legs
of a dinosaur that's dead on the ground
but thrashing yet, the message

not received at the farthermost outposts

MODEL-T: A SPIN AROUND THE COUNTRYSIDE

In science fiction, time continuums slip
against each other like plate tectonics,
there are timequakes, and a man might wake
five thousand years away. I don't believe that

quite, but I do believe this antique automobile crank
repeats the arm
of an ancient Egyptian temple dancer
angled in formulaic bas-relief. And

when Miss Simplicity Jean McCall
of Oak Grove, Michigan looked up one day
from the candling of eggs to witness this amazing
speed and commotion for the first time in her

history and ours, she saw the present
drive straight and clattering into the future
without one how-ya-doin' wave toward her basket and oil lamp,
and her hands itched to dance on the wheel.

MARCH. HALT. KNEEL. SHOOT. [REPEAT.]

There isn't any disorder, only
an order we can't see. For

instance, the British militia, lined up
like so many red encyclopedia volumes

—facing an enemy country's blue or green
arrangement of soldiers in a similar line across a field.

Yes. And then?

And then they were shipped to America
where the enemy sniped from trees.

SONG: HERE

Here's a harp of rib bones from the Upper Magdalenian.
Here's a tool-cut pebble from the Middle Pleistocene.
Here's a fish like a grate, and its mate, from a pit of the Devonian.
Here's a pair of ticket stubs from the Lower Mezzanine.

HISTORY: COUPLES

BENJAMIN WATERHOUSE HAWKINS

The "Freudian" reconstruction of Dickinson's work,
the "Marxist" reconstruction, the "feminist" . . . what
a day of colloquia! That night, late,
when he returns home, she's already asleep
in bed below the poster: James Webb telescope
corsages of starburst fire . . . so immeasurably far and alien,
in comparison they make the moon that strokes her flank
an intimate, familiar presence. Now,

beside her, watching her breathe, he understands
how anything we know of one another
is a best-guess reconstruction from the evidence:
subjective and, in part, a wish.

• • •

I met a man who worked for NASA
digitally coloring the James Webb pictures: "Not, of course,
to falsify. Let's say 'to interpret them for easier
acceptance.'" Searing iodine-red, viridian,
electric salmon. . . . So earlier, when I wrote "corsage"?
—much of that's his doing, just as some of it's
my own fund of perception and available words.
The same of Benjamin Waterhouse Hawkins,

who emerged in 1850 as the leading recreator
of Paleozoic-era specimens for museums in America and London
(in fact he worked with the man, Sir Richard Owens,

who coined the word *dinosauria*). Some of his larger models
were thirty tons. A dinner for twenty-one people
was held in the brand-new belly of one of Hawkins's iguanodons,
the party getting swozzled and singing chummily
into the dawn, from its capacious gut. All of that body

was smartly (and yet fallibly) conjectural. The bones
are fact; the rest, an expert's inference
around the bones. The lips and the hips
and the tenderest individuations . . . these are what,
exactly, time dissolves away from a skeleton,
then leaves it for the wind to whistle through.
Against that vision now, the man you met
in our opening scene is joining the moon
in lightly stroking the skin of the woman next to him:
the give, and the resistance, and the perishable
warmth: "soft tissue," paleontologists say,
each with a dream—but with a differing dream—
of the body's perfect existence.

THE POWER OF LESS

Surrounded and outnumbered by superior forces,
Confederate general Nathan Bedford Forrest still demanded
that the enemy surrender to him: and as he negotiated
with his Union foe, he had his two artillery pieces circling
past a clearing in the trees until they multiplied
two dozen times, and ditto his straggle of foot troops:
"and the Union commander surrendered his fifteen hundred men
to a rebel battalion of less than half that size."
                                                      And

the bough of a tree in the backyard dark
compacts the otherwise limitless immensity of "air" to something
in our range: a soulful, low
bassoon note.
                Looking "back" "down" from a point
in outer space, the solar system must be small
that way, a cluster like the grindstones
in an owl's crop.
                    And on the dot called Earth,
in something so arbitrary as "1986," in Austin, Texas,
in the house up the hill on Grooms, a woman is curled to a shape
that signals hard refusal, on that bed I remember
clearly even thirty-six years later. Such a tiny theater
for all of that clatter and acrid smoke and war-cry
as we continued to battle over whether or not
she secedes from the union.

THE CIVIL WAR

Twin brothers in the same house
with the same good looks and fears and friends
and crazyass stuff with the ladies and dreams
of knocking 'em dead in the world of business, kiddo.
And it happens. One becomes the latest CEO of Technolink,
with the schoolteacher wife, and one does and then redoes
the accounts books for the Mob and has seen a thing
or two you don't want to know. You've watched
that movie, read that book.
                              Today in the museum
there's a plum on the branch of a tree in China in 1650
so round that it makes the space that's meant as the air
conformingly round, and *so* bright in its lace of dew
that the dragonflies, even, diminish; on another
branch of the same tree is a plum that's withered.
The couple below it, studying it, then tired of it:
she yanks him by the hand to the Nineteenth Century Room
and you can tell by a subtle hesitation his heart
is in going outside for a smoke.

WHAT EVOLUTION REQUIRES

Benjamin Franklin thought that if he could be preserved in a vat of Madeira wine he would have liked very much to see what the world was like in a century or two.

—Jill Lepore, The New Yorker

    We all can tell the marriage is going, idiomatically,
south. Their party merriment, even: in molecules
of its pepsin and uterine lining and gamma globulin,
a sourness is brooding. In the way the lipstick smiles
independent of her lips; the way his handshake keeps on
bobbing like an oil pump long after the well's gone dry.
Is this what evolution requires?—testing the species,
strengthening the species, through adversity?
Is this what evolution demands
of these friends of mine? Up here today
the plains states shoulder into a blast of February wind
like bison attempting to patience out the storm,
hunkered and stolid and miserable. A siren
on the streets of my city is muffled by the snowfall
to mosquito whine—tiny, like the seed
of a woe still waiting for a future in which to flower.
On this winter day when the sky is an adamant gray,
I create a momentous event,

    and shatter the vat, and then decant Ben Franklin back
to walking, talking life. I think I'm more amazed than he is
that the dubious science of wineogenics (Madeira division)

works.
      Not that
he *isn't* astonished; once his wobbly gait is firm
and his bifocals polished (he lets us know what mastermind
first thought of those) he's full of breathy gogglement,
almost *anything* can do it. An out-of-date electric can opener
is as magic to him as the internet—*electric!* And look,
look, over there, an electric pencil sharpener! For him, they're all
the progeny of his wondrous kite: just show him a cord
and an "on" switch, and he's dancing some jiggy quadrille-step
like a lucky child at Christmas. "I desire to see this
whole new world!" We drive (*a car!*) to the shopping mall,
the trailer courts, the crafts museums, the strip clubs, oh
he's thrilled to see the great apotheosis of his own brain-child,
the Post Office, and I buy him stamps with the hundred-dollar bill
that sports his portrait. "An occasion for flying golden pennants
and winding a maypole!" he shouts and twirls. It's on

the way back that we stop at my two friends' house
so he can meet them. One more instance
of my famously bad judgment. She's as crumpled
as a wadded-up fast food receipt, she's sitting at the fireplace
emitting a wail of anger and bereavement that was already old
in front of the gates of Nineveh, old even
in the waters of the Flood. And he's at the window, staring
toward some spot that's really inside him,
where the puppet theater of Guilt and Accusation is performing
its endless, mesmerizing pantomime. It's now

that Franklin sighs, and asks for help in walking gingerly back

to the car on the ice-slick pavement.
In the grand salons of Paris where the *philosophes*
and their witty worldly paramours talk science and art,
and in the insufficiently sheltering housing of the Negro slaves,
and in the parlors of Federal power
as well as on the whorehouse steps,
at the churches, the wharves, the apprentices' ball . . .

he's witnessed this future a thousand times.

THE CLEANSING

Cilley had died . . . Mary had rejected him. . . .
And so they joined the miasmatic company of ghosts
that swirled his head and drizzled
into his writing. On July 23 of 1838, Hawthorne,
thirty-four and requiring quiet and cleansing, journeyed
from Salem by coach and train, to the thick-wooded
ridges and culverts of North Adams; and
on his first afternoon, having registered at the inn, he
hiked a narrow road through leaf-light, to a stream,
and stripped, and stretched out at full, in what he happily called
the "brawling waters." He would need this all his life.
"One dip into the salt-sea would be worth more
than a whole week's soaking," he'd later complain of that stream,
though would submerge himself once or twice daily.

. . .

Also, entering the realm of the dead is a matter of water:
wizened Charon, poling his dark, Plutonian raft,
the little dogteeth waves of the river nibbling its sides.
And reentering, back to the land of the living? . . . a bottle
of water was set at the stoop of our front door. I was
—what? thirteen? fourteen? Death was new to me; all of its
confronting and euphemizing rituals, new to me. And
I watched—weary down to the filament, yes, but even so,
dumbly attentive—as my father tilted it, singing out
the Hebrew in his much grief-crinkled voice, and symbolically
rinsed from his hands the casket-touch,

the first skirled dust, the last adhesive dander,
of his mother's burial: *now* we could cross the sill,
and commence our week of ritual mourning.

...

"A huge pile of cotton bales, as high as a house. . . . Barrels
of molasses, casks of linseed oil, iron in bars. . . . Long Wharf
is devoted to ponderous, evil-smelling, inelegant
necessaries of life." In another three years, he and Sophia
will marry. For now, she stays behind in Salem. Hawthorne
notes his days away in tallies of salt and of coal,
a "measurer" at the Boston Customs House. He calms
the tirades of the work gangs. He counts gulls for sheep
in his boardinghouse bed. Some days the fog's as gray as soot,
as thick. And when his mail is delivered
at the docks, he quickly pockets away Sophia's:
"I always feel as if your letters were too sacred to be read
in the midst of people—and (you will smile) I never read them
without first washing my hands."

TALK: THREE COUPLES

It isn't easy, figuring the likeliest psychology
of prehistoric tribes: the extant clues are few
and coveted by a dozen different sciences, and
the necessary energy for linking empathetically with a mind
so different is vast and draining, so that
by the end of a shift— *Oh jeezus,*
she interrupts, you just try linking empathetically every day
all day with a four- and a six-year-old,
if you want draining, if you want different minds.

       . . .

She was walking the beach, around dusk, the sun
already an orange fist on the water. A dolphin
started talking to her, it worked itself
as close as it could to the shoreline, and it talked to her:
past lives, and spirit wisdom, wonderful wonderful things.
What's he going to say? It's late, he's tired, tomorrow
he starts a new project. He's an exoterran biologist,
his job is imagining possible forms of carbon-based life
on other planets, and ways of communicating with them.

       . . .

She brought some smaller samples home: the petroglyphs
her dig unearthed that morning! And he wants,
he really *wants*, to look at these dumped-out rocks
with similar excitement. But at the Crisis Center

that afternoon—have you ever spent time questioning
a thirteen-year-old runaway who lives beneath a lean-to
where the hookers bring their slam-bam johns? . . .
. . . this glyph, that glyph, she's explaining.
Already a stoniness settles between them.

ZERO: TERROR AND LULLABYE

"If an electron were the size of a four-door car," etc.
The point is: nothing; it's almost all nothing
in there, in an atom, it's emptiness and dots.
Of course the solar system the same.
No wonder we need to believe in our various constructs:
God, and art, and all of the rest . . . otherwise,
without a central fetish, we'd be nothing but
a few connected dots inside a vacuum. Maybe
we've always suspected; always tried to ignore
the whine of zero in our ears . . . but isn't it worse,
now, *knowing?* Don't we sometimes wish that physics
had stopped at the door to the twentieth century,
thought hard, turned around, and drove back home
to its scrapers and beakers and bowls?

. . .

Einstein was *shikker*—drunk. He couldn't be
half so funny otherwise, or loud: he'd demonstrated
the speed of light in a crazy chicken-waddling trot
around the table. Bohr, as well: pernod had somehow
inflated both the amount and the pitch of his speech.
A nut house! Finally, however, their guests
had left—a little lurchingly—and they were alone
with the emptied plates and the emptied steins
and one another. The Curies: Pierre and Marie.
There was no need to talk; they were comfortable
with just their own two true, familiar bodies

on the sofa, in a silence that went out of them
and into the sky past Pluto, into a night
they shaped without even one word.

"Y'CALL SOMEPLACE PARADISE,
KISS IT GOODBYE."

—The Eagles, *The Last Resort*

In this faded fifteenth century *Expulsion*, everything
fleshily pink and gardenly green is seen to point
awayward: every tendril is inflexible with that
directive, every mossy root; and the brook; and
especially the arms of the angels like those flocks of tools
at the head of how-to diagrams, that carry
the eye off the page with their honed, honed tips. That's where
they're heading, the man and the woman: off the page.
The gray man and gray woman. Into the nothing-gray
off the page. It's the color of what you have left
after wringing a rag—the water that gets thrown out.
And over everything: the crazemarks
of the varnish and the paint—the timeworn wizenlines of art—
that remind me today of nothing so much

as the hairnets *de rigeuer* for the 1950's dimestore workers
serving my BLT (*"On toasted white!"*—as if
that were special) or gooping-out grilled cheese. I was five.
Things really did cost a dime or a nickel, including of course
(if you wanted, I guess, to emulate the look) a card of four
of the hairnets, sportily illustrated with a smiling woman
whose pixie coif was topped by exactly that fashion touch.
It all comes back in a dizzying circle
powered by thousands of gerbil wheels: the arc-and-plash
in the plastic fountain of orangeade; a couple (look sixteen

or so) in a smoochy romp up the lingerie aisle; the cap guns
and their red rows of prosciutto-like spirals of caps;
the cheap colognes, and the hosiery always just one day ahead
of a run; the spiritless parakeet-trill. Late afternoon,

I remember, that couple was told in no uncertain terms
to leave. I *think* I remember. They made "a ruckus"
—was that it? Or is it—trying now to fine-tune seventy
intervening years—that they were interracial? Would I even
have noticed that, then? And she was pregnant. Or was she?
Or was it the clumsy bulge of shoplifted goods? What's clear,
beyond revision over time, is those hairnetted guardians sternly
thumping the couple into the street, then lining up
—a wall of grim and unified refusal—at the door, and
my mother yanking me away as if this scene might harm me,
yanking me home to a world apart from these
confused transgressions. Seventy years ago. . . . The buckaroos
pajamas. The creaks of a house at night. What did *I* know?
—I was five, and even my terrors were innocent.

MIRRORS FOR THE WORLD OF HUMAN DOING

Autumn:
in the self-set, silent burning in the heart
of the heart-shaped leaf, we see
the self-consuming fires in our own hearts.

In the catcher's-mitt-of-a-cradle
that the new gorilla mother makes,
delicately, of her hands;
in the leisurely bowl-bottom swoop of a gull;
in the remora's glutinous clamp . . .
so many metaphors
for us, what we're like, what we do to each other.
Even in objects:
the waist of the ukulele.
Weather, even:
on a calm day during the Civil War,
and one when he allows himself some optimism,
Whitman observes, "As the President came out
on the capital portico, a curious little white cloud
. . . appeared like a hovering bird, right over him."

. . .

Is it because the park is the same park
that today, when I look at three appraising grackles
surrounding a dead squirrel, slowly circling it,
taking stock of their options (maybe
an eye would easily peck out, maybe a damp and rubbery sinew)

I remember last week—not far from this squirrel,
where the grass ends at a row of boulders—
a medical examiner, a detective, and a photographer
in their slow deliberate walk around
the body of a teenage boy
on the ground, his arms spread out
as if he were signaling with invisible flags.
Three grackles / three investigators . . .
how can we ever see those birds

as anything other than mirrors for the world
of human doing? The leopard. The ibis. The newt.
We'd need to think of them from before
we *called* them grackle, leopard, ibis, newt;
before the concept of symbol. Of course
by now that's impossible.

. . .

In the news this morning: excited ichthyologists
have determined that the Greenland shark,
although "belittled as sluggish, dim-witted, and homely,"
wins the prize for "the planet's
longest-lived vertebrate": estimates
for "one enormous female" (they can be "longer
than a station wagon") range from 270 years
to 390. "That could make her birth date
in the era of Rembrandt and Galileo."

I try to imagine facing that face
without intervention; Elizabeth Bishop attempts this

in "The Fish," and D.H. Lawrence, in his poems
about fish, and a snake, and others—flowers, even.
It can't be done. It can't be done
since even just the word "face" is the imposition
of our world onto that other.

When I look at my idea of this fish, that I take
from a color high-res photograph of this fish…
it's not unlike what Galileo might have intuited
on the roof, as the breezes broke over the railing,
and the aromas and clamors of everyday life diminished
in his awareness, and the stars appeared
in the "lenses-tube" he steadied on a tripod:
he was looking backwards into time.

I think I've seen the face of this fish
below the surface of Rembrandt's pale, doughy face
in the later self-portraits. He's done
for tonight—the paint needs to dry—
and, after he stretches the stiffness out
of his back and arms, and puffs
a tired breath from his cheeks, he walks
—a little sluggishly—upstairs to kiss the missus.

THE STORY OF MY WIFE'S BOW

Gilgamesh wasn't the first to search for immortality
(his are simply the baked clay tablets chance has provided).
Most certainly he wasn't the last
(gene splicing, CRISPR technology, etc.).
Here's some lumber (it's going to be the new hot dance club
on the corner; strobe lights, deejay stage).
Only yesterday that lumber was Gilgamesh's boat.
I remember my wife, at her art show opening,
taking a modest bow.
She was the elements of the universe,
performing one more encore.

RESPONSIBLE FOR

A friend is on vacation, and my wife
is charged with picking her lettuce
and two zucchini. It reminds me

loosely of the service I've read about
founded by some atheists: they'll continue
to walk, feed, groom the pets of those

who get transported by the Rapture
to another world. It's like a will:
one day I'll be gone, but in my absence I

desire that [fill in the blank] continue.
See that my poetry survives me.
Care for the goldfish. Pass along my DNA

and its gifts with fidelity. . . . In a way
we've all been charged to act as substitutes
for those who have preceded us,

and left us. Just to breathe the air
is a stewardship. We must be careful
and diligent. We must go leaf by leaf,

and join my wife beside the heaped-up bowl,
the piling green, the overspilling ever-present
beauty we're responsible for.

HISTORY: SNAPSHOTS, 3

. . .

Oh a clock is so full
of its minutes
—it's like reaching into a pouch
in a fish where the roe goes on forever.

A CLOCK

In one adventure, the stalwarts of the Time Patrol
recalibrate their dials, and travel back
to ancient Rome, as Nero's burning it. In another
they travel into the future and witness
the third of the Nanobot Wars. But there's
another way, and it's easier: just staying
still in your life, you're moving
into tomorrow. *That* machine won't stop its journey
even when the heart and brain of its passenger stop.
It keeps on using the newly released abundance
of atoms for fuel. In that sense, everything that exists
is a clock: A brick. A great love. A war. A child.
How easily only a shadow
pares our hours away on the sundial.

COULD DO WORSE

All of her life she was known for her stony,
unyielding martinet character—until
at the end she started to hum her way
through her remaining days, in the key of *mellow*.
Maybe it was a means of providing accompaniment

to the husky background whistling
the cancer scored into her lungs.
In any case, she was beloved by then,
by her family, by the hospital staff.
And also, in a tomb from the thirteenth century:

a flute that was fashioned delicately
from the tibia of a swan. These days, the more
I hear my politicians yammering—some,
jackhammering—their bullshit
vows and rationales, the more

I see how we could do worse
than to be repurposed for music.

REMNANTS

The confetti left after the bachelorette party.
The leftover wood from the whittlers' competition
that was used to jam open the jaws
of a buried vampire in the village's cemetery.
The sweet-but-muskily-pungent molecules of onion
still on the fingertips of the chef.
There was a Big Bang, out of Nothing, and
some of its recombined units of energy
bear your name for now and are reading this.

. . .

You may call these bedsheets
if you want—but the experts in sex and in anger
can recognize them for a fossil.

. . .

Out of the sheep, its gut.
Out of the gut, these strings.
And in the hands of the dutiful child practicing
at his music . . . a kind of bleating resumes.

SOME FIFTY YEARS

The weeping willow shoot was, what?—two inches
years ago. So many years that its documentation
is in a first-generation Polaroid exposure.
Now it leans over their fence

like a waterfall frozen in time—so huge,
it's less a tree and more its own
entire ecosystem. Lesson:
the largest door might open

to the smallest knock:
a pipette's drip of plankton; a pixel; a virus; the lovely
oil-sheen of a pubic hair
not even as wide as a fingerprint whorl.
Or, for the former trombonist, seated up front
in the audience at the symphony:
one wafted whiff of valve oil, and

she's back on stage—on stage some fifty years ago—
with the fluid fingers-of-then inside the gnarled
arthritic fingers-of-now, releasing lavish music
in the concert hall like a lighter-than-air gas
floating her,
floating her back and away.

THE YEAR IS 1997. THE "STARDUSTERS" HAVE ALREADY CONQUERED VENUS, MARS AND THE MOON. JUPITER IS THEIR NEXT GOAL.

—dust jacket copy for Frederic Brown's
The Lights in the Sky Are Stars (1953)

I know that Frederic Brown is wrong; but I have inside knowledge:
I live in 2022. I'm writing this in 2022, a fraught, bedraggled,
Earthbound 2022 that Brown could never have imagined, it's so
mundane in its wishes and crises. Merely sixty-nine years distant
on a linear scale, Brown is truly more in tune with the age
of the legendary sea captains, DeSoto, Magellan, Balboa.
There's a watchface that explains this, and it has no numbers,
only twelve amoebas on its surface, swimming, joining, parting
by whim. When X e-mails me her marriage complaints . . . I'm sorry,
I care about her, but a squiggling of the amoebas says it's 1972
and my own first marriage is falling apart. My wife and I are at
a Chinese New Years celebration, two of over 100 raucous partygoers
in the gaudy, sinuous Dragon, that waggles
its wavy, meandering way—its zigzag, maxicurlicuey way—
in a twisty maze of itself through the streets of the city.
Hey-hey-hey and whoop-de-doo—but I'm sad
up here in the fire-bearded and goggle-eyed head,
and I think that she's more likely executing a festive cha-cha
back in the tail. We're so separate—again. So far apart,
though both here in the body of the same great beast.

SO LATE

it's almost early;
and a delivery truck, for reasons
as dark as spaces in between the stars,
drives backwards on this downtown street.
Backwards.
Maybe this is the truck that delivers
cartons of carded hairnets;
rabbit-ear TV antennas;
and typewriter key replacement parts;
and newspapers—hey, remember them?
News! On paper! The headline on the top one
of this plastic-banded pile says
a man has just walked on the moon.

IN THE YELLOW FALL OF WATTAGE

Some men are never freshly shaved,
yet never bearded. Waking up in the morning,
making love or pining over love not made,
at the office, in church, at the races,
wherever . . . they're stubbled, stubbled eternally.
It's like the pencils

my father used, fussing his account books
for the company every night in our basement.
I never saw one whole and new,
I never saw one worn to the point of uselessness.
It was always a stub,
hard-working in the yellow fall of wattage.

Maybe the stars are that. They aren't
the original, bodiless Big Bang field of energy.
But they're not yet a nova or black hole.
They're like . . . they're like stubble,
radiant stubble up there. It's late;
my father sighs, and lightly runs a hand over his jaw.

NARROWS

How many stories about my father precede the final story, his death? *One* thousand? *Ten*? His garish salesman's laugh and his simple nobility. Passover *seders*. My high school dating. His first diagnosis, sending me into a night-long Lethe of bourbon-on-the-rocks. Say fifty thousand, all of it backstory now. But on the day we all convened at my mother's house, after the funeral, in the psychic blur of hours before the official *kaddish* prayers could be intoned, there was only an island of saddened numbness, unconnected to the planet and its narratives. Nothing registered. Birds out the window, the telephone and its shrill intrusions, whatever that was on the TV screen, can someone answer the door please, neighbors with casserole dishes like buckets in a fire brigade intended to douse our grief, turn down the television, the thought of the intolerably heavy presence of casket wood, some traffic noise leaked in from a parallel universe, where was his laugh *now*—now that we needed it, the way that attention narrows at moments like this and blocks out the rest of the world, what's that on the TV and who really cares, a neighbor's yapping dog, the sun now lowering itself to the horizon like a hand declaring it's folding its cards. That's it. That's the story I'm telling you. Oh—and that TV image, shown endlessly? "Challenger" something; a backstory.

BECAUSE LOVE IS A TIMELESS AND DISTANCELESS CIRCLE, WE'LL ALL MEET IN ITS CENTER

—Irving Goldbarth, d. January 1986

Sometimes I think: if I'm lucky, it will end
the way it once began:

*Morning. I wake. The first light,
in its nurse's whites, is holding me*

up for my father's young nod of approval.

HISTORY: FOUR NARRATIVES

MARY AND MARY AND MARY

A woman is asking her patient to read
the bottom line of the eye chart. A woman
is skillfully spooning the renal gland
out of a warm, still-kicking
mountain deer (it's used
in the best perfumes). A man
is briskly tapping needles
into the pads of flesh beneath the fingernails
of someone who won't divulge the necessary
information. And *that* man
won't talk, that man refuses to talk,
you filthy cocksuckers, He Won't Talk!
A married couple (straight or gay,
it doesn't matter) is on the porch
enjoying a lemonade. God wants

to understand them. All of them.
Everybody, God wants an intimate understanding
of everybody. That's why He thought up
Jesus, of course. So that Jesus could teach Him
our ways,
our glories, our everyday ho-hum bingo games,
our depravities. That's quite a burden.
The cross he dragged up the hill
might be a symbol of early-onset aging
caused by the burden of knowledge like that.

. . .

And since "chimpanzees and humans
are genetically 95 to 99 percent
the same"—where does it end,
this explaining? How complicated it is
for even the son of God!
How difficult, how impossible,
for us, stuck in the middle
of being us, to make a pronouncement
on even our everyday face in the bedroom mirror
with certainty.

. . .

Poet Anselm Hollo passes along the tale that,
after Mary Magdalene's body was cremated,
they discovered the tip of her nose remained
intact and perfect: Jesus, they say, had kissed her there.
He'd have, it seems, based on the record, consorted
("hung out," "chilled") with her kind of people
equitably—camp followers,
roughnecks, pilferers, fake beggars
and mountebanks, "good time girls,"
the sneakers into tents for reasons
lusty or thievish—as well as the deluded minions
of Baal and Ahura Mazda. He was,
after all, on Earth on a mission,
providing a kind
of empathy reconnaissance for the Lord.

There must have been nights
in the heat, in the sand, in the complex of homo sapiens itch,
when he acquired areas of knowledge,
dark and driven,
the Bible is circumspectly
mum about.

. . .

"Nothing human
is alien to me": Terence, philosopher/playwright
centuries B.C. Oh really?
Nothing? No one? Even

Leosbani Pino Lopez, who
over four months swallowed—and had
removed from his stomach—"nail clippers,
scissors, steel fragments, glass
and seven stones"? Even cult leader
Shin Ok-ju (who looks
like a stylish, bespectacled librarian);
her followers were ordered to beat each other, savagely,
to the point—in one not atypical case—
of "trauma to the brain" . . . even her?
The man arrested at Heathrow
for attempting to smuggle "two vulture eggs
in a body belt" (they happened to hatch
in transit) and "19 other eggs
from various birds of prey"? even him?
Or this: A woman (we'll call her Mary)

senses the air in the room become
. . . tenanted, become another kind of air
that makes another kind of room,
another kind of space than the merely
Terran and three-dimensional, and a voice
that she hears not only with her ears
but her marrow, announces (and this
creates a joy in her beyond
what our species evolved to receive)
that she will bear the child of God.
Ideally, yes: even that.
Even her.

Somewhere a father is weeping,
unashamedly, copiously, above the coffin
his son is in—his son
who was only out playing at ball-and-stick
along the contested border.
Maybe Jesus needs to channel this sorrow
upward to God, so He can know
how to act when the time comes.

The moon has seen so much now
from so many of us—almost
nothing is hidden—it's no wonder
once a month she needs to turn her face
back into the darkness,

renewing her tolerance
for our endlessly repellent,

hilarious, numinous, despicable, miraculous
multiplicity.

⋯

a woman is setting up the telemetric device
she hopes will capture a ghost a woman is
delivering sextuplets a woman is shitfaced
on her knees on the lawn with a .45 in her fist
a man is setting the bowl of ancestor rice
in front of the row of ancestor skulls a woman
is studying the 3-D scans of thousands
of beaks (the kite, the puffin, the boatbill)
a man is performing CPR a man is creating CGI
a man is numbing his palms for the crucifixion
reenactment they're everywhere they're
all of the time whether we feel any true simpático
or not they're here the way electrical current
is here ubiquitously even if we have nothing
plugged into the outlet

⋯

July 15, 1822.
The beach along that coast—Shelley's body
was found near Via Reggio, not far
from where the boat went down in storm and fog—
is blisteringly hot (and I mean that
literally: Trelawney says "the loose sand
scorched our feet"), so the heat from the furnace

Trelawney's ordered constructed adds its own
aggressive pinch of misery
to this sad day. What remains
of the poet—the corpse that's famously recognizable
by only the books left in its jacket pockets—is found

in its beachy grave by the sound
("dull hollow," Trelawney says) of an iron mattock
striking the skull; and "the corpse
was removed entire into the furnace. [It]
fell open and the heart was laid bare. . . . As the back
of the head rested on the red-hot bottom bars of the furnace,
the brains literally seethed, bubbled and boiled
as in a cauldron. But what surprised us all was
that the heart remained entire." Trelawney's hand
is "severely burnt" in opportunely snatching this precious
relic out of the flames; which, as you perhaps know,
he presents as a memento to Mary Wollstonecraft Shelley
—a Frankensteinian touch—and which she
treasures for an undisclosed number of years
as a keepsake. *Not* a scene from my life

or yours: but how instructive
and borders-expanding, to project
ourselves onto that beach, with that heat,
or hovering near the desk in Mary Shelley's study,
the heart in its lacquered reliquary.

...

For all I know, somebody dug his arms
up past the elbows into the still-warm greasy char
of Mary Magdalene's cremated remains.
For all I know, the tips of her fingers were there,
like small pink sea creatures scattered in the ash;
or her toes; because—for all I know, or you know—Jesus
may have kissed her affectionately there

and imparted eternity to those nubbins of flesh.
For all I know—and why not?—someone
may have left the scene of her cremation
with the intact ball of her left breast
carefully wrapped in a silk cloth, Jesus
having expanded his Father's understanding,
through his kisses there,
of human lips and desires.

DISCARDS

1. The Junkshop of Scientific Speculation

faces a neighborhood that, like all of the clockwork models
inside it, ran down long ago. A central door divides
two windowed show displays.
                              In one, a medieval
"goose tree" bears its poultry flora—some,
just sprouted, the size of lightbulbs, almost completely
transparent; others, larger, hanging like IV bags on a rack;
and a few of these milkying in color, turbid, albumeny,
as mapped in capillaries as a weary gaze,
in later stages showing thin damp feathering and
the tiny excrescent beginnings of beak and webs; then
finally the two black seeds near the stem take on the softer
unguent look of living eyes, and the wings stir: *flutter*
isn't the word yet, no, but like the gills
of certain torpid fish, these budge and shut, and
budge and shut, with the languor of moving through
oil or dream. Eventually they'll tussle
free, flap rapturously about the trunk,
like eggwhites being frenzied together, then
launch their V attuned to whatever chromosomal
star-chart we "now" "know" winks irresistibly in
those planetarium skulls. . . .
                              The other window
holds a single three-inch vial of—*krebíozen*, I think
it was called, and whatever the name and the FDA
approval, one day in the early 60's it didn't
undo the noduled mess the cancer made of auntie Regina's

brain, and I was twelve, and my mother was visibly
112 with lamentation, with cursing our share of this
almondine liquid that after all was no snakeoil shamster's
twaddle, but somebody's honest tested attempt at healing.
"Yeah, well I saw her today, she shook like a leaf, she drooled,"
my mother said, and she looked close to that
herself. "I don't know. They're upping her krebzíozen."
Here it is, a color darker than straw
but lighter than tannic—slender glassy finger
raised in saying "stop," but nothing stops,
my aunt kept dying until the dirty job was done. And
even so, if we could judge by just intention . . . seen
in *that* light, there's
a beauty to it deeper than its ornamental gleam.
                                        O

seen in *that* light, there's a beauty to all of these congregate vials,
retorts, beakers, cruets, ewers. . . . O
here are liquid quintessences of the famous Four Humours
every barbersurgeon, curate, philosopher, wag, and physick
swore by, once—the once of centuries—and now
they're relegated to these stubby containers something like that set
of different flavored syrups you get at the pancake house.
Here's an ounce of pure phlogiston. And here's its kin
exquisitude, the "ether" Descartes said invisibly
filled The Void, it was to gas as silk to burlap.
Here's a jar of "effluxion," it used to vehicle
light from the sun to the Earth. And here, a shotglass-worth
of Buckland's Flood—yes, William Buckland,
the Dean of Westminster, who lavished his prodigious talent
on proving the theory of "one Worldwide Deluge," in part determined by
his studies of "diluvial sediment," some of which

ribbons slitherily around in here like tooth gunk
in a dentist's expectoration cup. . . .
You'll even find, on the brick floor in back, the burnt-out match
of Jefferson's idea: personal liberty, applied by creatures
flawed but essentially noble. It's been dropped here,
it seems, by this manikin marked PHRENOLOGY,
whose skull is dotted-lined like the side of a steer
in a butcher shop poster. There was a brief flame, *pfft!*,
that shivered like a leaf, but that was long ago. A leaf, then
just this dimness.

2. Cleansing

"The God of the Yellow River in ancient times claimed each year a beautiful maiden as his bride. After a period of feasting the girl was put on a marriage bed in a boat, and launched in the river. In modern times the hesitation in some provinces to rescue drowning persons is attributed to an unwillingness to deprive the River of his sacrifice."

—R. D. Jameson

But *Tashlich* is simpler, if similarly
offertory in spirit. Every year, in spring,
the Jews of the village gather
at the bank of the river, or maybe on a bridge
above the river, and with little ceremony
—sometimes no more than a token benediction
and some singing—fling their year's sins
into its onrush. There are stories of local variants:
a place where tiny rafts of cork are set in the water,

a single candle on each. But everywhere, in any case,
the idea of cleansing, of bearing away the corpse
of the symbolically-rejected, holds true. In Chicago
when I was a child, we'd walk—as if the Bible Itself
ordained the details of it just this way—
to the drainage canal, where we'd lighten ourselves
of the breadcrumbs and lint of our misdeeds.

. . .

All of those poems in which
time is like a river.
All of those songs in which rivers of tears are
called forth, flooding the plains with grief.
All of those nights in its current, all of those
dreams of being carried back
by the gills, to our start in the sea.
It's a wonder we're not yet clean.
It's a wonder it's never quite
the final flensing-knife we long for.

. . .

Afterwards, I remember, there would be treats—not candy,
a boring traditional mix of almonds and raisins; we'd walk home
quietly—presumably, the adults feeling the halls of their conscience
freshly-swept. I don't remember much more than that.
My sins? the ethical fallings-away I might have thought
I launched like tiny paper boats into those dark braids? . . .
I can't guess. Perhaps I wouldn't have guessed them
even then, felt guilty over *not* possessing guilt, and put

a nine-year-old's small dramatized embellishments on some happenstance,
to give it ritual value, as the crowd about me
cast down sins like people feeding pigeons
and the first of the season's opened drainage flowers
sweetened the evening air.

...

And my sins since then? No
chainsaw murders. No international terrorism.
But even so—like anyone, no matter
our intentions—there's a history of hurts I've provided
about the size of pistachios, sorrows
gleaming like bolts and wingnuts in a hardware bin,
that I've left in the lives of people I love, and of this
I'm ashamed, though some are so old
by now, their modes of pain and disappointment are out of fashion.
They existed, though; if each could be given its slice of cork
and candle, they would be a floating
show of flickers heading into distance, with
such momentary heat and life, we might hear the ghost
of a shriek of some victim
thrown to the gods of the waters,
so that the rest of us could get on with our lives.

3. Buttoned-Tight Suit

"Tomorrow I'm going to take the stove to the doctor's."
Stove for *bus.* And at this seemingly comic
pronouncement from auntie Regina, my mother began the first

soft lowing of adult grief I remember hearing.
There had been tears before, and anger, but nothing like this
unstoppable ratchet-catching. We could hear it,
my sister and I, behind our bedroom door—no,
through the bedroom door, our ears were pressed against it,
clammy hammering hearts. I stared at the lush fake coonfur
on my plastic Davy Crockett wallet, as if in Zen attempt
to reorder the world by the strength of my fixedness alone,
but my aunt kept jumping the tracks of her brain
and my sister—Livia was seven—kept dancing
painfully in place as if the floor were wired. Later,
there was more of this wretched waiting,
in the hospital lobby (children weren't allowed in the wards)
while everything in the world seemed to soften
out of its strictest defining, and the krebíozen failed
day by day. It did no good, the clenched fists
of that layer-of-me I was back then did no good
. . . all of the praying was ineffectual. Well
there's a time for strength, for immediate facing
into the psyche's tripped alarms. And there's a time
for running through the aisles of the Junkshop, past
its antique maps of a foursquare Earth, its cabinets
of impervious pool-ball atoms, its gryphons,
its grungy tanks of medicinal leeches, running
through the clutter, through the dear slough, to the last niche,
curling up there through the long night
with the homunculus in his buttoned-tight suit.

"A MUSEUM, OF SORTS, FOR ERRORS."

—Nicols Fox, *Against the Machine*

1.

The docent is late (she took a wrong turn
off the interstate), and in the wrong gallery.
Amy—that's her name. The tag she grabbed on the run
from out of the office's tags box
says Lavonda. "This way, please"—just now
she's leading them to the newly renovated
Hall of Celebrity What-Were-They-*Thinking?* (i.e.,
Britney Spears's kwikee Vegas marriage that lasted fifty-five hours).
Somehow, though, they wind up in the crowded Rotunda
of Scientific Fallacies, at the glass case
where a homunculus is unrolled under the pitiless wattage,
adhesive and fishy, looking as raw
as an infant's leg in the burn ward. Once
we grew from this: yes, all of us. We grew from this
below the blemishless sun
as it circled around the Earth.

2.

Alexander Hamilton: "Why yes, of course I accept
this invitation to duel with Mr. Aaron Burr"
—*what* was he thinking? Based on nothing more
than pen pal correspondence for four-and-a-half years,
Tracy Cope, a British citizen, flew to Asheville, North Carolina,
and there "she wed James Lewis Morgan at the prison
where he's on death row for the murder of a woman
he stabbed 48 times with a broken malt liquor bottle";
now the newlyweds "will get to see each other
for 90 minutes a week, with a wall of glass between them."
What is she *thinking*? Science
thrives on error—that's the way it arrives
at the shape of the truth—and evidently so
do all of us, out battling through the overmuch, the undertow,
the hurlyburlyesque of human lives.
To evolution, the dodo wasn't "a failed experiment";
it simply was its dodo self for its dodo while
—maybe that can help us bring a sprinkling of affection
to our dead-end one-night stands and crashed investments.
So there *should* be this museum that displays
the fall of hasty, failed paint-and-plaster chemistry
that flaked for all those centuries from the very air
in the room of da Vinci's *Last Supper*; or the Zip-a-Talk,
that intended to carry "electrically-conducted conversation"
through "the universal etherium." . . . "And here,"
our docent says, in sadness tempered by a year
of Monday-through-Friday familiarity, "is the bullet,"
or more accurately the .54-caliber ball—one ounce

of ugly intention—that, a little after 7 a.m. on July 11, 1804,
on a narrow ledge about twenty feet over the Hudson
near Weehawken, New Jersey, exited the smoothbore pistol
aimed by Aaron Burr—who was then Vice President
of the United States—and struck Alexander Hamilton
on the right side, making a two-inch hole above his hip,
fracturing his rib cage, ricocheting off the rib, up
through the liver and the diaphragm, and then
splintering the second lumbar vertebra and,
thirty-three hours later, resulting in Hamilton's death.
Yes, here it is: on a sky-blue velveteen pillow
edged in amber frogging: something like the dot
some archeologist might retrieve from over the "i"
in "bad idea."

3.

Bad ideas.
According to Gordon S. Wood's researches, "Hamilton,
acutely conscious of his honor and sensitive to every slight,
was the principal in eleven affairs of honor
during his lifetime." This is one of the factoids
Amy knows, who takes her docent responsibilities
seriously, and some nights—for a unit
of comparison—takes them home.
Example: Marrying Ed was a bad idea,
the dickbrain rat. The baby was an accident.
The divorce was a good idea—of course—but sloppily done,
and to her financial disservice. Now they only speak
to each other through lawyers: less effective, even,
than futzing around with the electro-coiled helmets
and Frankenstein laboratory attachments of the Zip-a-Talk.
But there are bad ideas, she thinks—"innocent bad ideas,"
in that they only harm the consensual—and *baaad* ideas:
George W. Bush's invasion of Iraq will one day merit
a place in the Hall of Mendacious Ineptitude in ways
her own small-term miscalculations of the heart
and the crotch will not. And the baby,
the "accident": it turns out that her daughter is
what saves her from self-pity and abandon: like tonight:
when she retrieves her from the sitter,
there's a burble-up of formula that's dried now
to a lazy seafoam over her chin, and everything else
no matter how global and dire takes its place
in the shade of this wonder. One exhibit at the museum

is those blind albino cave fish we've discovered
in various similar sunless eco-niches scattered about the planet;
"errors"—if everyday salmon and trout
are "correct"; and yet you *know* they turn
and dart and home like compass needles,
with a bioexpertise exactly appropriate
to their sightless lives. That's *her!*—somehow,
against the grain of "should," she's made her life work.
Other women (as she warms up a bottle of formula,
she warms to her topic) shouldn't be allowed to have children.
The radio story this morning . . . someone
held her baby's leg to a grill of live embers
"to teach it a lesson"—which it must be contemplating
in the burn ward now, the leg a sticky length
of pain, and the equal pain of the lesson
more invisibly relegated to a sealed mouth
in the back of the brain, for the rest of its life.
That woman.
What was she thinking?

4.

The architectural plan was gorgeous.
And the shell as it was constructed at the top of the hill
(for they wanted their library complex to be "the crown
of the university neighborhood") was correspondingly
gorgeous. Even, maybe especially, the opening ribbon-cutting
champagne celebration that afternoon: sublime.
And the following morning, rainy, slippery, revealed
that the entire building had slid down to the base of the hill,
the weight of the books they had just placed on the shelving
. . . not accounted for.

. . .

On a blunder scale of 1 to 10 (as narratives go)
the mullet was surely a 7. We can see
that now. And yet those people got sex
and held political office and played the mandolin
and spoke with God and collected ceramic thimbles
like anyone else. It's here,
a representative one, in Case 11-C:
a sort of roadkill-looking raccoony item,
limp and weather-streaked and formerly blowdried.
Here, in 14-A: this lumpy dull-gray platter is a model
of the flat Earth. It's a silent panegyric
to a (literally) outmoded world. And next to it
in 14-B, and looking like its long-lost twin: a model
in clay of astronomer Fred Hoyle's theory
of steady-state expansion, that's since lost out

to the rival Big Bang vision. (He was a brilliant seer,
although his obituary in *Nature* said
that he "put his name to much rubbish"). Over in 69-South,
a perfect one: a stupid night;
of stupid love; that somebody captured on Betamax.
And one day maybe the possibilities
we so eagerly spin and luster and jam
our hopes inside of will be on display:
a translucent and blobby mock-up of memes
("They thought there were *memes?*"), a long list
of "political correctness" on a sanitized scroll,
and the bowl of plastic spaghetti above its burnished plaque,
String Theory. And even so,
we muddle along, as they muddled along (and begat,
and begat, until we were here), religiously
and scientifically lifting their pouches of lilac and chamomile
to their noses to ward off the Plague, and ditto
pendants of garlic for vampires, ditto woven eyes
to counter the "evil eye" of the Jews, while overhead
the planets of the Ptolemaic sky revolved and oversaw
the machinations and lice of kings,
the sputtering joys and monumental sufferings and lice of the rabble,
as if their solar system had been Banged out from the mind of God
from zero to forever.

. . .

And now Amy slips into her jammies . . . oh crap,
she forgot to leave this name tag
back in the front desk drawer—this ID
bearing her error-name. Well, whatever.
The baby is gooing in its bassinet, and Amy
wipes some dribble from the sweet chin
of this sweet mistake—as pleased, somehow,
as if her life had been planned for this
from the beginning. "Way to go," she thinks
to herself, with a wry grin
recognizing how crazy-lucky things
turn out sometimes. "Way to go, Lavonda."

5.

She was thinking she didn't have enough money.
Thinking she didn't have enough sex. Thinking
she was fat or skinny or out of weed and thinking
how she loved the baby, the little-her, and hated
the baby, the drain, the burden, the never-ever-ending,
and she wanted it to shut up, and the phone kept ringing,
and she thought this guy she knew was interested
or something, and the rent, and the pain, and the baby's cry,
and it wouldn't stop, and it needed to learn
what's right from wrong, and the phone, and the noise,
and its leg, and the embers.
That's what she was thinking.

6.

It may be a mistake
to bring myself into the text of the poem at its last.
I'll chance that. We'd be paralyzed
if every possible fumble required days
of gingerly hesitation. It's a mistake
to believe that anything's "solid"; really matter
—us, a pebble, a Happy Meal toy, a stadium—is emptiness.
And even so, in bed tonight beside my wife
I stroke her back as if it's really there,
as if the glide of hand along the roll of skin
were really there and really mattered.
I'm wrong, I know. And yet I go on stroking anyway.
As if the pleasure outweighed the void.
As if we care.
As if there were a place where even I belonged.

NOTES TOWARD TWO POEMS ARGUING EACH OTHER, AND TOWARD A CODA THAT ATTEMPTS TO FAVOR ONE

Notes Toward the First

Bryce just nixed his deal with the dude in Argentina, who originally was going to manufacture and distribute the collectible alien figurines Bryce designed (with the lure of one quarter of a gameboard ["get all four!"] on back of the blister pack). "He wanted a limited run of these at a really high retail price-point. No go. I want cheap and millions of these. I'm thinking . . . " (I wish I could imitate his rosy exuberance) ". . . Pokémon!" The Grail. The ultimate. Alpha and Omega. "So I'll find someone else. I'll patent it, it'll be my second patent." The things one hears, from an employee in the back room of a comics shop.

I ask about the first patent. "I was nine. My great-uncle was a patent attorney, a senior partner in a powerhouse New York firm. He patented 'Bryce's Dice & Slice.' He was a wonderful man. He did cartoons for *The New Yorker* AND he worked on the Manhattan Project."

"He was a physicist?"

"He was the guy . . . they'd tell him the parts that were needed and he'd find them and deliver them."

So he was a high-level gofer, maybe the highest level imaginable, for the making of the atom bomb. In 1945 the War Department awarded him a special citation, for "services contributing to the successful conclusion of World War II."

My wife looked all of this up and it's true, and in fact there's even more true. A-plus gofer cred aside, his Manhattan Project connection came about (this, from the *New York Times* obituary archives) because in addition to graduating "from NY School of Law," he'd already earned "a degree in metallurgical engineering" (Columbia, 1938) and put that know-how to work at International Nickel "where he developed a procedure for making nickel sheet of the right porosity to separate uranium 235 from uranium 238."

Anything else? I'm glad you asked. In 1930 "he was an Eastern Conference Champion pole vaulter," and later "held the Metropolitan Intercollegiate Title in pole vaulting."

Amazing lives. But aren't they all? Bill Bryson says, in his book *The Body: A Guide for Occupants,* "Altogether it takes 7 billion billion billion (that's 7,000,000,000,000,000,000,000,000,0000, or 7 octillion) atoms to make you. . . . Your lungs, smoothed out, would cover a tennis court, and the airways within them would stretch nearly from coast to coast." A meter of DNA is packed inside every cell—and if *all* of the DNA from *all* of the cells of your body formed a single strand, "it would stretch ten billion miles, to beyond Pluto. Think of it: there is enough of you to leave the solar system." Who *isn't* a poster boy or girl or trans for "astonishing"?

• • •

From 1889 to as late as 1941 (when she was profiled in *The New Yorker*), Mary Pfeiffer collected two thousand feet of spider silk every year for use as crosshairs in gunsights and high-end optical instruments. Clients included the military and well-known manufacturers of surveyors' scopes. At a minimum, then, her one-woman cottage industry extruded 10,400 feet of spider silk, and while that won't get you anywhere near Pluto, it's enough to widen my eyes in immediate wonder. "Once every summer she would enlist a group of boys [Hoboken, New Jersey] to scour the marshland for the critters, for each of which she paid fifteen cents."

In 1939, as Pfeiffer's business was winding down, Nan Songer of Yucaipa, California took up the torch. From an issue of *Cabinet:* "Songer's silk production technique was so sophisticated that, with the encouragement of the US Bureau of Standards, she began offering web to precise specifications from 'extra-heavy' (1/5000th of an inch) to 'extra-fine' (1/50,000th of an inch). For the most sensitive applications, she marketed the silk of week-old baby spiders, which at 1/500,000th of an inch was virtually invisible."

Anyone else? I'm glad you asked *that* too.

Einstein. Van Gogh. Marie Curie. Gandhi. Rosa Parks. Etc.

Shanda wobbled out of the trick's hotel at 4 a.m. and into the BMW, and two outlaw brothers from Aces East, who she owed, who she'd pissed off royally with her twitchy ass and her lips-filler sneer, were waiting around a corner, and when they skreeled away, they left behind nine bullet holes decorating the car that it turns out she didn't own anyway. As usual, she fled the scene without so much as one scratch or a mosquito bite to mar her miles of fresh-peach-melba on-display look-at-me skin.

And she carried the baby (the baby bundled up and Shanda in nothing more than a peekaboo nightie under a flannel shirt) a mile to the clinic, on a day of four inches of snow with more coming down and a wind that weaponized every flake. Like everything else, "a girl's gotta do what a girl's gotta do," so she did it.

• • •

Ral Kumar of Uttar Pradesh, India, while relaxing at home, was bitten by a snake, which he bit back, killing it: "He chewed it to pieces," his father reported. A seven-year-old Indian boy named Ravindran "was found to have 526 teeth inside his jaw," some approaching—as you'd well imagine—merely pinhead size, but all with "a small crown, enamel and a small root." Thea Alba, billed as "The Woman with 10 Brains," could write sentences with both hands simultaneously, in French, German, and English, and was similarly simul-ambidextrous in drawing landscapes with colored chalks: "In the course of a long career she exhibited for Maxim Gorky, Wilhelm II, and Woodrow Wilson."

Nineteenth century fairground performer Sarah Biffin "born without hands, feet, or legs" painted landscapes, portraits, and miniatures, some done on fine china ("she placed the brush in her mouth and supported it with her shoulder"), and in 1822 "she was appointed miniature painter to his Royal Highness, the Prince of Orange." In 1809, Richard Brinsley Sheridan watched his Drury Lane Theater burn to the ground, and was heard to remark, "Cannot a man take a glass of wine by his own fireside?"—a shining example of sangfroid tested successfully by circumstance. A Scotsman, Gregor MacGregor, "came to London in 1822 as the official representative of an imaginary country he called Poyais and marketed £200,000 of its bonds, as well as sold fictitious land there." Would you spend a substantial part of your lifetime studying "the reproductive apparatus of mealworms"? Me neither. But Nettie Stevens did, and in 1905 at Bryn Mawr College she discovered thereby the Y chromosome ("and—her crucial insight—realized that it seemed to have a role in determining sex").

Etc. Endless etc.

• • •

But how about the Ho-Hum Humdrum poster couple as dull as iceberg lettuce sitting placidly across from you in the restaurant, Mr. Bland and Mrs. Empty, with his 9-to-5 cubicle job and monthly bowling, with her neighborhood newsletter column? Their *clichés* are clichés. Bill Bryson however serves to remind us that in them, too, a dot of brain the size of a grain of sand "could hold two thousand tetrabytes of information, enough to store all the movies ever made, trailers included." Their bodies, as much as Gandhi's or Curie's or Shanda's, make a million red blood cells "every second or so," and each will orbit inside them 150,000 times before its demise.

The Van Gogh *Starry Night* inside their planetarium craniums is pulsing with as much neural dazzle as Einstein's was. Who are *we*, to condescend to whatever portion of courage has them facing another day each day? Who *isn't* a perfect poster boy or girl or trans for "astonishing"?

. . .

Notes Toward the Second

It's Christmas day. My friend Dan is touring Germany. Evidently his idea of sending a Yuletide hello through my phone is to gift me, first, a photo of the Museum of Victims of War—a gray and somber space, appropriately—and second, a photo of (equally somber and gray) the Memorial to the Murdered Jews of Europe: 2,700 somber-gray coffin-shaped blocks of stone. Vast. A hamlet of namelessness, of death as blank-faced oblongs.

There's something . . . *necessary* here, in the designing of this memorial as cubic tonnage. Otherwise the lesson is that our lives are dandelion fluff that the planet puffs out into the void. Our lives are petals in a storm, or less, are sawdust, or less, are drops of water mindlessly shook off the rump of the world and gone in an eye-blink.

We all know the number: six million murdered Jews. Add Gypsies on top of that, and Poles, and homosexuals. The numbers of *any* genocide are greater than our heads can comprehend. The murdered as numerous as stars. As if we looked into the sky and every star was a dead star. Many are, of course, though their light is first reaching us now. In *that* astronomy, light is little more than a monument to the departed.

But statistics, being beyond us, can't affect us in the way that individual cases can. For example, here are specimens in the Nazis' Hall of Medical Horrors. The man who had a thin glass tube inserted up his penis, and then they cracked it in half. The woman who had an electric eel jammed into her vagina, head-first, tail writhing out of her. There's a room out of which a child's face and head were carried separately.

Nazis. The bad guys. However the paper today, my *USA Today* for January 3, 2020 says (as part of a year-plus investigation done in concert with the *Milwaukee Journal Sentinel*, and including a Senate Armed Services Committee report) that a United States military raid in Azizabad, Afghanistan in 2008 was "touted as a victory. A high-value Taliban target was killed; the collateral damage was minimal; the village was grateful.

"None of it was true.

"The Taliban commander escaped. Dozens of civilians were dead in the rubble, including as many as 60 children. The population rioted.

"A doctor recorded a cellphone video to document the dead faces, freckled with shrapnel and blood, coated with dust and debris. Some were Afghan men of fighting age but most were women and children. Tazi was 3 years old. Maida was 2. Zia, 1.

"'It was wholesale slaughter' [said] David McDonnell . . . who oversaw mine clearing projects."

So *we* were the bad guys. Or, to be fair, in a world of mazed complexities beyond control and understanding, we were the bad guys *too*.

We disappear in flakes, transparent flakes as thin as breath, and they're hurled to the whirlwinds and scattered beyond reclaiming. The universe seems not to care. We were crazy to think that it does, that somehow we're more to the universe than any other temporary and random collection of atoms, a maggot's, a strand of scum's on the pond. There go the Zia atoms! *Who?*

Even without the military to help out, even just day to day. Bill Bryson: "We shed skin copiously, almost carelessly. . . . Run a finger along a dusty shelf, and you are in large part clearing a path through fragments of your former self." They mingle with motes from silverfish and your smelly old man neighbor. The universe doesn't think the telescoping upward of your DNA past Pluto is miraculous. The universe doesn't think *Pluto* is miraculous, or the blinding blaze of the sun, or the Son, or our songs or science or angels.

And it's not just war that peels us like a gummy residue off of the Earth. One-on-one works too. The woman raped in the park two miles from here and then—aah, this is the connoisseur touch!—her body set on fire. Or two miles in the other direction, the baby momma who suffocated the twins while they were sleeping because, depending on who you believe, the man she'd been cheating with (the *other* baby momma's baby daddy) "didn't like children" OR "God wanted them for a sacrifice."

The very stones in the vacant lots of this city ought to be shrieking such abominations unto the subtle ears of Heaven. They're not. That's only poetry blather. They're stones—inert. They don't care.

And the car crash. And the cancer stories. Lord, I'm sick of the cancer stories, tired of hearing the word and then walking fearfully through the rest of my day as if I'd been warned about an invasion of Huns or Cossacks or thugees down from the hills, *look out, there's a cancer around the corner!* Earthquake. Tsunami. Guy with a gun in the movie theater, the church, the mosque, the synagogue, woman stepping onto the bus with a home-made explosive strapped to her waist, or an explosive put together by her sleeper cell—*do-it-yourself is all the rage*—and the dude with a facebook post of his arsenal and the dog he's just shot held up as if it's a trophy he's proud of. The reeds at the river are bowing their heads, but not for this, no, not for us, and it isn't really "bowing," that's just me talking. The reeds don't care, or the river.

If there were only *one* slave ever, the atoms of oxygen and hydrogen in water should tear apart in grievous rage, but in fact in 1860 there were

3,963,760 black slaves suffering in the American South. And slavery has been ubiquitous: "At one time Algiers had held as many as 25,000 white Christians as slaves"—Paul Johnson. Geld them, whip them everywhere including their privates, annihilate their names. And yet the oxygen and hydrogen don't wring in consternation like hands. People are lost to the maelstrom but the waters continue to flow just fine.

And Patsy? This is a made-up name but an actual person. Patsy, who was smart and loved and talented and retroprogressive fashionable? Because she was a physician she knew which pills would be most efficient and exactly how many to use and she lined them up on the edge of her desk like a tiny firing squad, and she issued them the order; the darkness she'd been carrying in her head was the darkness she entered.

As John Aubrey said around 1650, "Many worthy Names and Notions are swallowed-up in oblivion." Oh yes. Oh very certainly yes.

Sappho (in the Richard Lattimore translation): "You will die and be still, never shall memory be left of you / after this, nor regret when you are gone. . . / you must drift with a ghost's fluttering wings, one of the darkened dead."

Oh yes amen oh yes amen.

• • •

Rough Notes for a Coda

Still, in another fragment Sappho says, "But I claim there will be some who remember us when we are gone."

I've been trying to write about John Francis, the next door neighbors' boy, who has averaged one heart surgery for every year of his life: he's four. They're back from Chicago today, where the last— and they're hoping the *last*—of his operations took place. His ready, unclouded smile and his energetically goofy Jedi spinning-around with a plastic dollar-store lightsaber . . . you would never guess the recent cardiac history.

I've been trying to write that poem, but my parents keep intervening. And why not? Death is a powerful force, but it's never yet kept its citizenry from appearing in poems. In *Gilgamesh* that's true, and in the latest *American Poetry Review*. The dead walk into our living brains as effortlessly as neutrinos pass through concrete.

And they loved me, and my sister, unstintingly. That too is a powerful force.

Often when I've gone walking at night—merely to clear the day's rubble out of my thoughts—they've seemed to accompany me. The starlight too is a memory (I've addressed this before), a memory over many millions of years.

In the summer, we'd pay at a farm to go blueberry picking, or blackberries. Winter: get out the snow chains for the tires!

There's a section in *Roughing It* where Mark Twain describes how sensitive are the scales in an assaying office: "If you weigh a two-inch scrap of paper on them and then write your name on the paper with a coarse, soft pencil and weigh it again, the scales will take marked notice of the addition."

That's what the stars say, although not in words. A name—against all of the evidence to the contrary—has a weight, and counts.

We hammer stories into the sky, the Bull, the Maid, the Swan, and they attain a version of permanence. Even the dailymost stories are up there. A dipper. A field of rushes. A belt.

Irving Goldbarth. Fannie Seligman Goldbarth. John Francis Clark.

Sometimes that poem seems almost to come together, at last, from its many pull-apart pieces. Sometimes it slips away. I walk under the stars . . . I come back in and write. . . .

You know what it's like, when everything in you is teasing you with its glimmering possibility of completion, when the energy feels perfectly in vibratory alignment with the matter in the universe, and the words seem to tumble out on their own, because even "just sitting quietly, doing nothing at all, your brain churns through more information in thirty seconds than the Hubble Space Telescope has processed in thirty years," amazing me, amazing you, amazing language, and we write our poems pretending they might be undying, we want them to be that good, that electric with *pow!*, we want them to be so (there's no way I can say it better than Bryce's way, in Bryce's voice, with Bryce's unvarying confidence in a clement future about to come true), we want them to be *so . . . Pokémon!*

"ANACHRONISMS

"ANACHRONISMS

abound in [Shakespeare's] plays. He has ancient Egyptians playing billiards."

—Bill Bryson, *Shakespeare: the World as Stage*

1.

Are *you* surprised when our Congresspeople
gasconade and pettifog?

Have you had your knee buckles polished?
Is the chataqua about to begin?

>halberd
greaves
portcullis
tabard
syrinx
sistrum
ramillie
pattens
reticule
lioncel
vavasor
brougham
escutcheon
buttonhook
goose quill pen

Some days my head seems merely a delivery system
carrying around these words and their referent objects,
out of their context, into the future

that you and I call "today."
I think of a glacier with a shrub inside it,
a wand-like bone detached from a mammoth inside it,
and bearing these prehistoric treasures
inch by steady inch, until they're finally deposited
many hundreds of miles—and centuries—farther up the line.

Here,
the massive Stonehenge boulder-columns;
there,
the toe bone of a deer,
robustly carved with chevrons
51,000 years ago by a deft Neanderthal artist.
I bring them into the Shop-4-Less,
I scatter them and their long-gone ilk
prodigiously to mark my way up the interstate.
This lidded porcelain bowl
the barberphysician stored his leeches in. . . .
A page of my grandpa Louie's
daily Yiddish-language newspaper, roused by the wind
in my brain, and flapping into the distance like a sea gull. . . .
And let's not forget the future

that's already traveled backwards
and takes shape in our minds as a premonition:

the future of bionic cyborgandroidthink
is already retrocolonizing our consciousness;
the future of technology's "predictive power"
coupling with online marketing to monetize
our neural-level decision-making
is already retrocolonizing our consciousness;
the future of species extinctions and ice cap disappearances
is already retrocolonizing our consciousness;
these scenarios rattle around in our thoughts

amid the "smart pills," "personal jet-pack travel,"
and—that big one—Heaven.

The lesson?—time is confusing. Agitating.
There isn't enough. And there's too much.

Maybe we need to calm down with a quaff of posset.
Maybe, if the chataqua is finished, this is the moment
to pass around the calumet for peace.
Maybe with festive background accompaniment
(who doesn't like a last dance?)
from the sackbut and the dudelsack.

2.

A sheet of newspaper lifts in the wind
and flaps away, like a sea gull, over the harbor....
The man who will one day be my grandfather,
Louis Seligman ("blesséd man" is what it means),
stands in the cattle-crowd of immigrants   *1
at Ellis Island (this would be about 1903)
and idly studies the mix of birds and airborne litter
gliding through the sky; and sighs; and sits on his only possession,
a bundle of soiled clothes and toiletries; and waits
to be motioned over for the eye exam   *2
(if they thought you had trachoma, that was enough,
genug!, they sent you back over the ocean again
to face the clubs of the Tsar's enforcers).
He doesn't, at this moment, feel so very
blesséd at all. And yet, although he can't see

even an hour ahead, he'll successfully pass that test.
A brusque but kindly Yiddish-speaking volunteer
from the Hebrew Aid Society will deliver him
to the Accommodation Committee's tenement boardinghouse,   *3
and another volunteer will begin to explain to him
the rudiments: employment, traffic, how to negotiate
hooligans and police (not always easy to differentiate).
And here, you can have this, Louie, here
take it, the Yiddish-language *Forward*.
That's the direction Louie wants to go—forward. Ahead.   *4

Ahead in this new world. Every day that paper
presented "ahead"'s confusing array of vectors:

finance, gang wars, synagogue services, pool hall allure,
and letters of recent arrivals' *mitzvahs* and *tsooris*.
So much! And maybe somewhere out there
a woman would think this thin, green hank of a man
had a future. Maybe they would flirt
and court on the nighttime back alley fire escapes
where matches were made, and promises whispered.
They would have children.
Maybe a grandson.

. . .

Some unpacking:

*1 Fifteen thousand might arrive in a day, for day after day. The ferry between the island and the mainland shuttled continuously through twenty-four hours. Altogether, sixteen million people were processed here ("a sausage factory," said Georges Perec).

*2 It "hurts a little. It terrifies the children. Trachoma [is] the cause of more than half of the medical detentions" (Irving Howe, *World of Our Fathers*). If you were suspected of carrying it, your coat was chalked with the letter E and you were held over for further, and not always gentle, probing.

*3 Four to a room, or eight, or—why not?—fourteen: tenement living for newcomer Jews was barely tolerable. "An immigrant remembers a two-room apartment . . . containing parents, six children, and six boarders" (Irving Howe). The compulsion to rise in employment status (or to risk illegal money-making) was often just another face of the need for better lodging.

*4 Or more completely and formally, the *Jewish Daily Forward*. Or more correctly—that is, in Yiddish—the *Forverts*. It was a true microcosm: gossip and slander, populist politics, City Hall news, heartbreaking stories of everyday life in the sweatshops and on the streets, lampooning comic strips, influential Jewish intellectuals locking horns. By the late 20s/early 30s it had a formidable circulation of 275,000.

3.

—flipping quickly through this book
—page 183, a smartphone
with its screen completely covered
in emoticons
   blink-in blink-out
/ no, an ancient palm-sized
baked clay tablet
filled with cuneiform

—a rocket car
from the 25th century
   blink-in blink-out
/ no, a sketch
by Giovanni di Fontana
circa 1425 A.D.

"On October 22, 2021, the *Los Angeles Times* reported that on Thursday actor Alec Baldwin, while practicing on the set of *Rust* (being filmed at Bonanza Creek Ranch near Santa Fe, New Mexico), accidentally killed cinematographer Halyna Hutchins as she huddled around a monitor lining up her next camera shot. Unknown to Baldwin, the prop gun, which had been presented to him as 'cold,' i.e., empty of ammunition, was actually loaded with live rounds. The projectile whizzed past a camera operator but penetrated Hutchins, then continued through to non-fatally wound Joel Souza, the movie's director."
             —a social media post

blink-in blink-out

"In 1587 a visitor from the country wrote excitedly to his father about an unexpected event he had seen at a performance by the Admiral's Men: One actor had raised a musket to fire at another, but the musket ball 'missed the fellow he aimed at and killed a child, and a woman great with child forthwith, and hit another man in the head very sore.' . . . One wonders where they were hoping the musket ball *would* lodge."

—Bill Bryson, *Shakespeare: the World as Stage*

4.

Some words from the past
that are entering this Tuesday afternoon
through a vent in my head:
                         panopticon
                         hippocras
                         hornbook
                         frumenty
                         digisol
                         hoosegow
                         mugwumps
                         gat
Oh wait. Sorry, "digisol"
is from the future.
I don't know *what* it means.
I don't know *how* it got here.

Maybe I carried it back here
in a dream-state. Maybe everybody lives
in a congruency of multiple times.
Gordon Ng applied for a grant
and then, with devotion, immersed himself
in designing the "primate habitat" his grant described
and ordering the materials and the engineers,
and informed the press, informed his university department.
But the grant was denied. "I guess," he said,
"I got a little ahead of myself."

. . .

Looking back over my notes for this poem
(and I make no claim for my handwriting's legibility)
I see "Easter Island"
—those huge deific, sentinel heads—
blink-in blink-out
Ellis.

. . .

They say there's . . . what? . . . two? or four? percent
Neanderthal in our genome. And we carry it
into the present moment,
peripatetic time machines
(and descendants) that we are.
As for the energy of the Big Bang . . .
hi, we're here, we exist to carry that energy
into "now," as matter.

. . .

And a question: When *is* "the past" the past?
One former American GI in the trenches
of World War II remembers how easy it was
—how almost a psychological *mandate* it was—
for soldiers he sheltered with to imagine
future terrifying encounters with the enemy,
that almost never did happen; "this would not,
however, prevent their dreaming about it later,
perhaps for years, 'reliving' in dreams
the confrontation they never lived through originally."

. . .

I don't expect my work will survive to be read
by future generations. By that definition, you
—you reading this—you were there too
in the 2020 Covid pandemic:
the masks, the latex gloves and the hand sanitizer,
the mail left to air-out on the porch . . .
                              blink-in blink-out
"During the terrible smallpox epidemic of 1764,
when Boston became 'one great hospital,'
[John Adams] went to the city to be inoculated. . . .
[Abigail Adams] worried excessively and they corresponded
nearly every day, Adams reminding her to be sure
to have his letters 'smoked,' on the chance
they carried contamination."
—David McCullough, *John Adams*

. . .

Bill Bryson reports on Shakespeare's most
incomprehensible line (from the Quarto edition of 1608),
swithald footed thrice the old,
a nellthu night more and her nine fold.
"No one has ever got it close
to making convincing sense." My theory is
these words are from the future, and traveled back
by chrono-osmosis
to visit his in-love-with-language, capacious, curious brain.
They traveled back to him from the digisol.

. . .

In Edgar Rice Burroughs's *The Moon Maid*,
the protagonist philosophizes, "Keep in mind the theory
that there is no such thing as time
—that there is no past and no future." Or
the other theory, that everything is time,
is pure submicroscopic units of time in motion.

Confusing. Agitating.
Some nights, to clear my head, I need to walk . . .

5.

. . . out, into the kind of dusk that quiets
too much thinking. The busy whisks the wind makes
of the branches in the upper boughs
are still. The moon is waned to a tiny peel
of its earlier magnificence. Everything: calm.
Although walk long enough in the deepening,
accommodating dark, and you'll eventually arrive
at a small free-standing building
alive with the sounds of bustle and hustle, and neon-lit
with one word: BILLIARDS. Really, that's
too fancy. It's pool. Look through a window,
into this bright and noisy box of camaraderie.
A game is in progress. A team of ancient Egyptians
(yes, I said ancient Egyptians: just Google the look
of their headdresses, from some *National Geographic* story
on Tut) have decided to challenge all comers.
The click of the balls. The clinking of beer steins.
"Yo, Louie, ya lardass! Get a move on,
you're up!" And so that bless*é*d man
indeed steps from his bar stool
with a great unrushed aplomb,
and makes a show of brushing the dust of Ellis Island
from his jacket cuffs,
and steps to the table, lifts his cue
with a smooth, vaudevillian twirl, then
squints to sight down its length,
to strategize every trajectory,
every possible formulation and jot,
and holds one finger up as a joke, as if testing the wind,
and calls the shot.